Remembering Victoria

Remembering Victoria

A Tragic Nahuat Love Story

JAMES M. TAGGART

University of Texas Press ⟡ Austin

Requests for permission to reproduce material from this work should be sent to:
    Permissions
    University of Texas Press
    P.O. Box 7819
    Austin, TX 78713-7819
    www.utexas.edu/utpress/about/bpermission.html

♾ The paper used in this book meets the minimum requirements of ANSI/NISO
Z39.48-1992 (R1997) (Permanence of Paper).

Library of Congress Cataloging-in-Publication Data
Taggart, James M., 1941–
Remembering Victoria : a tragic Nahuat love story / James M. Taggart. — 1st ed.
    p.   cm.
Includes bibliographical references and index.
ISBN 978-0-292-71686-5 (cloth : alk. paper) —
ISBN 978-0-292-71687-2 (pbk. : alk. paper)
1. Nahuas—Wars—Mexico—Huitzilán de Serdán (Mexico) 2. Nahuas—
Violence against—Mexico—Huitzilán de Serdán. 3. Fratricide—Mexico—
Huitzilán de Serdán. 4. Huitzilán de Serdán (Mexico)—Social conditions.
5. Huitzilán de Serdán (Mexico)—Moral conditions. I. Title.
F1221.N3T35   2007
305.897′45207248—dc22
                                                                          2007020257

Contents

Preface **vii**

Chapter 1. Introduction **1**

Chapter 2. The Tragedy **11**

Chapter 3. Talcuaco **36**

Chapter 4. Fratricide **48**

Chapter 5. "Rabbit and Coyote" **65**

Chapter 6. Human Goodness **73**

Chapter 7. Nahueh **83**

Chapter 8. Love as Desire **95**

Chapter 9. Wife as Sister **104**

Chapter 10. Conclusions **113**

Notes **119**

Works Cited **129**

Index **137**

Preface

This book deals with a small civil war in which neighbor turned against neighbor in a community deep in the heart of the northern sierra of Puebla. Those who witnessed the events of this war spoke about acts of cruelty, vengeance, cowardice, bravery, heroism, and love. The war broke out in 1977, nine years after I went to Huitzilan de Serdán to start fieldwork in anthropology. At that time, Huitzilan had a large concentration of monolingual Nahuat speakers, who lived with a small number of Spanish-speaking mestizos whose ancestors had settled in the community in the late 1800s and early 1900s. Over the years, I have developed very close friendships with many of these Nahuat and mestizos, who always gave me, and my family, their warmth and generosity.

Using their words when possible, I have presented their story of a bloody struggle that left many dead and others grieving for them. Their small war was a microcosm of the problems occurring in the region as a whole. While some people acted badly during that war, I found tragedy but little evidence of organized evil. The Nahuat and the mestizos suffered tremendously during this period, but they also found within themselves the ability to rebuild their lives with love. It is to them that I dedicate this book.

Many people have contributed to this project, and I owe a special debt of gratitude to Nacho Angel Hernández, who told me his story about what happened to his wife, Victoria, and to him after I left Huitzilan in the spring of 1978. He spoke of the anger that swept through his community, and he spoke of the love he felt for Victoria, for his family, and for his community. He not only described how Huitzilan came apart, but he also told how the Nahuat could draw from their culture to put it back together. The people of Huitzilan have displayed a remarkable resiliency of the human spirit, which I hope will come through the pages of this book.

Many others have supported this project, and they include all of the Nahuat and the mestizos who generously gave me their accounts of what happened in Huitzilan. I also benefited from generous grants from the Wenner-Gren Foundation, the Andrew Mellon Foundation, the American Philosophical Society Penrose Fund, the National Science Foundation, and the stipend from the Lewis Audenreid Professorship in History and Archaeology of Franklin and Marshall College, which paid for my many trips to Huitzilan over the last thirty-eight years.

This book is based in part on my interpretation of Nahuat culture, which I had the opportunity to present, as the Directeur d'etudes invité, to the École Pratique des Hautes Études, Section des Sciences Religieuses, at the Sorbonne in May of 2002. I am grateful to Michel Graulich for inviting me and for sharing his insights into Nahua culture.

Several more people contributed to writing and revising this manuscript. They include Irene Aco Cortés, a Huitzilteca who now lives in Lancaster and who edited my Spanish translations of this work. I presented the translations to the people of Huitzilan who had contributed their testimonies of what happened in their community to make sure this book represents their views fairly and accurately. Margaret Hollenbach read two drafts of the English version of this manuscript and offered her excellent suggestions for how to show rather than tell what happened in Huitzilan. My beloved wife, Carole Counihan, also read two earlier drafts of the English version with her keen editorial eye and her high standards for clarity. Alan Sandstrom has given me constant encouragement to continue working with the Nahuat and wrote a very helpful prepublication review. An anonymous reviewer also offered excellent suggestions for how to make a book out of a manuscript. I am grateful to Paul Spragens for copyediting my manuscript and to Lynne Chapman for her editorial supervision. Finally, I thank Theresa May for believing in my work.

J. M. T.

Remembering Victoria

CHAPTER I

Introduction

On October 15, 1983, Victoria picked up her infant son and walked with her daughter across Huitzilan to pay her mother a visit. The next day, villagers found her body lying in a pool of blood, with her son attempting to nurse from his dead mother's breast. Victoria perished in the violence that broke out in 1977 when forty Nahuat men invaded and planted a cornfield on a cattle pasture known as Talcuaco. The word Talcuaco means in Nahuat "land above the community" and refers to a locality on the steep slopes above Huitzilan. It was a visible reminder that, a century before, Spanish-speaking mestizos had come into this predominantly indigenous community and converted cornfields into cattle pastures, sugarcane fields, and coffee orchards. It became the object of a dispute involving mestizos, and, after 1977, it turned into the symbol of a bloody war that left hundreds dead and forced many others to flee Huitzilan for good.

These events were beginning to unfold during the last year of a long-term fieldwork project on oral narratives that I began in 1968 and continued until 1978. I learned of Victoria's death after I had left Huitzilan. In 2003 I returned to find out how and why Victoria had died and what had happened to her husband, Nacho Angel. Nacho told his story in 2004; it is both a political and a personal chronicle of the events that began when mestizo leaders of the UCI appeared in Huitzilan in 1977. The UCI is an acronym for the Union of Independent Farmers, or Unión Campesina Independiente. The leaders reputedly came from the neighboring state of Veracruz to organize Nahuat and Totonac villagers in the northern sierra of Puebla into cooperatives that invaded uncultivated land, as in the episode in Huitzilan.

Nacho described how a deep political conflict erupted when the UCI leader Felipe Reyes appeared in his community. Felipe Reyes organized forty Nahuat men from Huitzilan into an armed cooperative that invaded both Talcuaco and Taltempan, another plot at the southern end of town. The later deliberate destruction of the UCI's cornfield caused them to attack and kill their enemies, and Nacho called their reaction the rage, or "cualayot." Nacho and Victoria were caught in the middle of the rage because her father and some of her brothers had joined the UCI, while Nacho had served in the town hall as justice of the peace when the violence was reaching its peak (1979–1981). The town hall president, a Nahuat, allegedly had collaborated with the mestizo who had humiliated the Nahuat in the UCI, by orchestrating the destruction of the Talcuaco cornfield; consequently, Nacho found he was on the UCI's hit list.

Telling His Story

Nacho told his story in Nahuat and in three stages over three days. On the first day he described the circumstances leading up to Victoria's death, their last days together, and his effort to get his children out of Huitzilan. On the second day Nacho told the story of his life from his earliest memories to his courtship of and marriage with Victoria. I asked him to tell me about his earlier life to fill in the pieces of his family's history missing from the account I had gathered many years earlier.

The third day took a surprising turn, as Nacho took it upon himself to describe the meaning of a ritual involving a flower tree, or "xochicuahuit," that I had described the Nahuat using in family ceremonies of baptism and marriage during the earlier fieldwork (1968–1978).[1] He told how the Nahuat could take action to restore the love and respect that temporarily disappeared from their community by carrying out these rituals. The flower tree is an adornment that may have a historical relationship to the mythic account of a pre-Hispanic goddess who picked a flower from the tree in the celestial realm of the gods, descended to earth, and gave birth to the corn plant.[2] When Nacho explained the contemporary meaning of the flower tree, he emphasized its role in spreading ties of human goodness (cualtacayot), or love (tazohtaliz) and respect (icnoyot).

His discussion of love on the last day of our three-day interview caused me to ponder what he and other Nahuat meant by love, or tazohtaliz. Nacho and other narrators had used this word in their oral narratives, and I had heard it in conversations, but it had not become a focus of my earlier studies. After listening to all three parts of his story, it became apparent to me that love, or tazohtaliz, was an important but overlooked concept in his culture. I wanted to know what he meant by love and understand his grief caused by the rage that tore through Huitzilan.

Narrative and Memory

Nacho said his story of what happened to Victoria and his love of and grief for her are a lesson, or neixcuitil, the word he had used earlier for all of the stories he and other Nahuat had told about the past. Many of those stories were about other people who lived in different times and places than the storyteller. Nacho's story of what happened to Victoria is his personal memory of what happened to him, and that makes his neixcuitil more like a testimony than a myth or a folktale. To emphasize that his story is his personal memory, he ended his three-day narration by saying: "I always remember." ("Siempre niquelnamiqui.") So his testimony is both a narrative (neixcuitil) and a memory (tēlnāmiquiliz).[3]

I shall attempt in this book to pin down Nacho's narrative of past events by anchoring his memory in what I know of him and his community since starting fieldwork in Huitzilan in 1968. Ricoeur reminds us, in his tour through Western philosophy, that the memory of past events is not the same thing as actually experiencing them when they happened.[4] Holocaust scholars such as Primo Levi are distrustful of testimonies for many reasons: survivors express a particular point of view; memories change; chronologies become confused; witnesses cannot see everything; and survivors are unusual because they lived while so many others died.[5]

Nacho's memories of anger and love are deeply entwined in his narrative, and I shall use different methods to pin them down. When dealing with the anger (Chapters 2 through 5), I shall draw on the testimonies of other survivors of the Talcuaco conflict. They include Nacho's oldest daughter and members of the family of the mestizo who took a conspicuous role in driving the UCI out of Huitzilan. Also included are witnesses who saw and heard things in Huitzilan that Nacho could not have seen because of his problems with the UCI, which forced him to go into exile shortly before Victoria died. These witnesses not only saw different events, they experienced and interpreted some of the same events differently. Their testimonies coincided with many of Nacho's recollections but also revealed how his memory of the rage was filtered through his particular position in his community and in accord with his personal history.

For interpreting Nacho's memory of loving and grieving for Victoria (Chapters 6 through 9), I shall draw on the Orpheus stories[6] that he had told earlier, first when courting Victoria and later after they had been married for several years and were raising their children. The Orpheus stories anticipated his experience of loving and then grieving for Victoria.[7] They are from the Native American Orpheus tradition, and they describe the loss a man feels when the woman he loves goes to the land of the dead.[8] Set against his 2004 reminiscences, the tales provide a glimpse into a Nahuat marriage over a period of thirty-four years.[9]

In the first Orpheus, he described a man loving a woman with an intense desire much like that of a young man who is about to marry the woman he is courting. In the second Orpheus, he represented a man loving a woman as a sister, much as a man and woman may become like a brother and sister after several years of marriage. His recollection of Victoria in 2004 reflects the more idealized love that a man has for a woman about whom he feels an intense grief. It also bears the stamp of experiences that took place between 1978 and her death in 1983. During those five years, Nacho and Victoria grew even closer as the conflict became more violent.

Love, or Tazohtaliz

Reports of fear and anger abound in accounts of the many large and small wars that have raged in Mexico and Central America.[10] Far fewer are the accounts of love and affection, which presumably are the emotions holding us together in our marriages, our families, and our communities. The Nahuat word for love, tazohtaliz, has many meanings, which will become apparent from a close examination of Nacho's narrative of remembering Victoria, his earlier Orpheus stories, and his explication of their meaning to him.[11] The contemporary Nahuat word for love, tazohtaliz, is closely related to the ancient Nahuatl term tlazohtlaliz, which appeared in Alonso de Molina's 1571 dictionary.[12] Molina said that tazo(h)tlaliz meant amor, the Spanish word for love, and gave no other definition.[13]

Alfredo López Austin explained that the ancient Nahuas[14] associated feelings such as tazohtaliz with the bodily centers of vital substances or animistic forces. The most important center was and continues to be the heart, or "yollo," which was the location of "vitality, knowledge, inclination, and feeling." Another center was the liver, or "elli," which was involved with love, desire, and cupidity, as well as anger and hate.[15]

Nacho added to López Austin's model by revealing how Nahuat talk about emotions also has a social referent. He told how the emotions associated with the animistic centers of the liver and the heart arose in particular social situations. During my earlier fieldwork (1968–1978), Nacho and many other Nahuat in Huitzilan described in their stories specific examples of behavior that is inconsiderate, or "ilihuiz," which came from the liver.[16] Ilihuiz refers to strong emotions, which, if acted upon, always end badly. When remembering Victoria in 2004, however, Nacho spoke more about the heart when talking about anger as well as love.[17] When recollecting how the violence arose leading to Victoria's death, he said that with anger "we make our hearts cold."[18] When explaining how he knew he loved Victoria, he said: "I felt I loved her because I felt it in my inside, in my heart."[19] He brought up the heart again when he described his grief after Victoria's death as "a great big wound to the heart."[20]

On these occasions, Nacho was remembering his feelings, and, as Wendy James reminds us, remembrance is where one can find an emotion expressed as a concept.[21] Nacho's concept of tazohtaliz was different from romantic love as expressed in the narratives I recorded in Spain.[22] The Spanish term for romantic love is "the illusion," or "la ilusión," and refers to the aura one feels as the most wonderful person in the eyes of another.[23]

Nacho and other Nahuat spoke differently about love and marriage than the Spaniards I had known in Spain. While Nahuat spoke of marrying for love, they also told cautionary tales warning men to control their desire lest they love women obsessively, leading them to a bad end. They spoke of the need for a man to moderate desire, an unruly form of tazohtaliz, with respect. All of Nacho's narratives—his tales of Orpheus and his memory of Victoria—reveal how he moderated his desire from the time of his courtship through his marriage and after his wife's death.

That Nacho would have a different notion about love and marriage than Spaniards should come as no surprise, given the very different historical antecedents of Nahua and Spanish culture. Noemí Quezada hypothesized that the sixteenth-century Nahuatl concept of tlazohtlaliz and the Spanish notion of amor were bound to be different because of the respective ideas about women in the two cultural traditions.[24] Nahuatl ideas about love were related to respect for the procreative powers of women, which the goddess Xochiquetzal personified in the myth of Tamoanchan. In that myth, Xochiquetzal picked a flower, representing sex, from a tree in the celestial realm of Tamoanchan, fell to earth, and gave birth to Cinteotl, from whose body sprouted many edible plants.[25] Several contemporary meanings of the word tlazohtlaliz (Nahuatl) or tazohtaliz (Nahuat) appear related to the symbolism in this myth. One is the tendency to associate women and food. The other is respect for the procreative powers of women who give birth to children who work to fill the family granary and turn raw ingredients into delicious meals. During my earlier fieldwork, many Nahuat in the northern sierra of Puebla told stories about feminine characters producing vast quantities of edible food from a single bean or kernel of corn.[26]

Nacho's Culture

Nacho's ideas about love and anger are the product of his communalistic culture, which has mixed Native Mesoamerican and Spanish antecedents. While few believe that today's Mesoamericans have retained their pre-Columbian culture in pure form, some scholars have recognized and described the continuities between the ancient cultures and contemporary Mesoamericans like Nacho. One continuity is that the Nahuat, like other Mesoamericans, continue to grow corn communally in their extended families, pooling the fruits of their labor in a granary from which women may draw according to need. Nacho grew up in one of the most stable extended families in Huitzilan, in which he and his brothers worked for more years pooling the fruits of their labor than other groups of brothers I had known during my earlier fieldwork (1968–1978). One sign of having grown up in this family is his style of narration, in which he presented himself as acted upon rather than as taking action, when describing the events leading up to Victoria's death. His narrative style is consistent with his notion of personhood, according to which acting autonomously is inconsistent with the communal organization of work in the extended family, where men pool the fruits of their labor to fill a common granary, which women use to feed their families. Nacho's notion of personhood is like that of many other Mesoamericans because he sees himself not as an independent individual but as one who, to borrow from Gary Gossen, is "*subject to the agency and will of others*, both human and supernatural."[27]

Particularly relevant for understanding Nacho's story of love and anger is June Nash's interpretation of ancient and contemporary Mesoamerica, important because she focused on the continuities as well as the changes in both Nahua and Mayan images of women. As Noemí Quezada reminds us, those images are important for understanding how a Nahuat man might love a woman. Nash begins with the observation that the religion of the ancient ceremonial center and city of Teotihuacan (A.D. 150–675) was based on the worship of a creator goddess similar to the spider woman of the Hopi. The creative powers of that goddess were undoubtedly related to her powers of procreation.

Nash notes that gender hierarchy increased among the pre-Columbian Nahuas, or Mexica, as they expanded their empire and became more militaristic in the middle 1400s. The trend toward gender hierarchy continued after the Spanish Conquest of 1521, but the importance of goddesses and their role in creation also continued and, in some cases, actually increased relative to what existed in the pre-Conquest Mexica empire.[28]

Historical Context

Nevertheless, the Nahuat of Huitzilan have faced a number of serious problems threatening their way of life. My earlier fieldwork during the ten years leading up to the arrival of the UCI in Huitzilan had revealed that the Nahuat were living under very great pressures—landlessness and ethnic domination—that had taken a toll on human relations. The lack of cheap land had made it very difficult for the Nahuat to produce the corn they needed for their granaries, and it had exacerbated old tensions and created new ones.[29] I saw considerable anger, or cualayot, particularly among men who were drinking. Nahuat gender relations seemed strained, measured by the images that men painted of women in their oral narratives. Their images were more negative than those in men's narratives I had recorded in Yaonáhuac, another Nahuat community in the northern sierra of Puebla. In Yaonáhuac, the distribution of land was more equitable, and the Nahuat were not under the direct domination of mestizos in their community.[30]

The differences between the images of women in the Huitzilan and the Yaonáhuac stories accord with a widespread pattern of domination bleeding the love out of the marriages in the dominated group.[31] The tension in marriage that showed up in the stories that men told about women was a symptom of splintering among the Nahuat that came to a head in the violence that surged when the UCI appeared and organized the invasion of the Talcuaco and Taltempan pastures.

The invasion of Talcuaco and Taltempan was part of a pattern that developed earlier in the Huasteca of Hidalgo in 1971[32] and spread south along the Gulf Coast to Huitzilan in the northern sierra of Puebla. The UCI was one of many groups with a Maoist ideology that attempted to address class inequalities by invading uncultivated land. The press reported that 250 land invasions throughout Mexico had taken place in 1977 and 1978 alone.[33] The UCI came to the northern sierra from Veracruz with the intention of organizing Nahuat, Nahuatl, and Totonac villagers to take over land without a title, as happened in Huitzilan. Its organizers first appeared in the neighboring community of Pahuatla, a one-hour walk from Huitzilan. After orchestrating a land invasion in that community, they came to Huitzilan, where a few UCI leaders organized about forty Nahuat men into a cooperative, and helped them arm and carry out the land invasions on two plots that were the objects of a dispute between two Spanish-speaking, or mestizo, families.

To understand what happened next in Huitzilan, it will help to realize that the UCI turned into a group of armed men who acted differently than some other groups of insurgents in Mexico and Guatemala in the 1970s and 1980s. Like the EZLN[34] of southeastern Mexico, also known as the Zapatistas, the UCI began with noble agrarian aims, invoking the memory of Emiliano Zapata by declaring in slogans and speeches that land belongs to those who work it. The UCI invasion of Talcuaco and Taltempan aimed to relieve landlessness, which had become a big problem by 1977. However, the UCI abandoned its agrarian aims after the destruction of the Talcuaco cornfield. The insurgents turned their anger on other Nahuat and a few mestizos whom they considered to be against them. Nacho said the Nahuat in the UCI were committing fratricide because they were killing other Nahuat. The fratricidal conflict was the complete collapse of a moral order that the Nahuat socialized into their children and tried to create through rituals.

Frans Schryer described earlier land invasions in the Huasteca of Hidalgo, not far from the northern sierra of Puebla, and provided a very thorough view of how they fit into the context of local and national politics of that period. He spent "a fair amount of time in the city of Huejutla in order to get slice-of-time snapshots of what was happening in the political headquarters of peasant organizations or in the homes of peasant leaders or local landowners who were influential on the regional or state level."[35] This book presents Nacho's story to complement Schryer's study by providing a personal perspective on the events that took place in Huitzilan.

The Value of Personal History

I turned to Nacho to find out what had happened in Huitzilan because we had worked together for a long time, and he knew me well and was willing to speak frankly about the events affecting him and his feelings about them. I had befriended both Nacho and Victoria in 1968, before they started courting each other in 1970. Victoria was a regular visitor in my home because she had befriended my former wife, Sharon, and she stopped by frequently on her way to visit her grandfather who lived just up the street. I had made Nacho's family an important case in my study of the family during the first stage of the earlier fieldwork. Nacho taught me Nahuat; he told me many stories; and years later he helped me correct my transcriptions of Nahuat stories I had recorded from him and from nine other narrators in Huitzilan between 1970 and 1978. I made regular, daily visits to Nacho and Victoria between 1973 and 1978 when doing fieldwork in Huitzilan, and enjoyed their warm hospitality, ate many of Victoria's delicious meals, and played with their children, Epifania and Alfonso.

Nacho's story is his personal history of the Nahuat struggle to hold onto their culture, which is largely invisible to all but a few specialists.[36] Judith Zur and Linda Green make a case for why personal histories are important for understanding how and why communities splinter in a small war, such as the one that broke out in Huitzilan.[37] Linda Green believes that anthropologists have maintained "a silence on suffering" by not focusing on particular individuals caught up in those wars, and this silence has prevented the understanding of "why internal violence happened in some communities and not in others."[38] Judith Zur adds that personal histories can reveal the "long-existing animosities and rivalry" that can break out into internal violence with some "locally significant event or change."[39] Nacho's story of the tragedy[40] (Chapter 2) and the testimonies of other Nahuat and mestizos (Chapters 3 and 4) reveal just how Huitzilan splintered along the lines of conflict rooted in the past, long before the UCI leader Felipe Reyes appeared in the northern sierra of Puebla in 1977.

As a war widower, Nacho complements the picture Zur and Green present of the suffering of war widows in Guatemala. He not only provides a masculine perspective on suffering, but he is also willing to talk openly about feelings of love and grief. To have feelings and to tell a story about them are two marks of Nacho's humanity,[41] and, in presenting his story, I hope readers can identify with his experiences. I am following the lead of Renato Rosaldo and Ruth Behar, who have urged anthropologists to write about feelings of grief to round out our picture of the human condition.[42] Nancy Chodorow has stressed the importance of personal histories because they help us understand more fully just what feelings are, how they are linked to specific experience, and how we give them meaning.[43] She is looking for the middle ground between the psychoanalytic view that feelings are drives and the constructionist view that they are created through language and ritual.[44] Nacho provided that kind of historical perspective on his own personal history as well as on that of his community during our association, which spans thirty-eight years. Nacho's story shows how, to borrow from Miles Richardson, we are cruel, we are magnificent, and we are loving in a particular Nahuat way.[45]

Writing Remembering Victoria

Nacho and I had many conversations between 2003 and 2006, in which he provided most of the information on which I base this book. I then embarked on writing in a way that would not put Nacho in a vulnerable position. The conflict involving the UCI is not over in Huitzilan. Newspaper articles and Internet sites continued to mention deaths attributable to that conflict in the year that Nacho decided to tell his tragic story of love and loss. We did not want anything potentially troublesome for him to appear in print, particularly in Mexico. So I wrote a first draft in English and translated it into Spanish, with the help of Irene Aco Cortés, a native of Huitzilan, and read it to Nacho. On that first reading, we decided to disguise the names of some of the people who took an important role in the Talcuaco conflict, and he suggested that I remove other portions for fear that they would come back to haunt him. I revised the manuscript with the changes he suggested and translated it into Spanish a second time with Irene Aco Cortés's help, and then read it to him a few months later. He suggested a few more changes and seemed satisfied with the result. In the chapters that follow, I describe the setting, and present Nacho's words and those of others in Huitzilan in the hope that you, the reader, will understand what happened in a beautiful but troubled community in the northern sierra of Puebla.

CHAPTER 2

The Tragedy

Most of the events in Nacho's story of the anger took place in Huitzilan, whose 2,273 Nahuat and 275 mestizos[1] arranged their houses in a narrow green valley in the interior of the northern sierra of Puebla. In 1968, the Nahuat and the mestizos had arranged their houses according to the contour of the land and without evidence of an urban plan, which one can find in other communities in the northern sierra of Puebla. Bernardo García Martínez found evidence in the colonial archives that the Nahuat of Huitzilan resisted the efforts of Church and civil authorities to resettle or congregate them in a neatly laid out town.[2] Zapotitlán just to the north and Tetela de Ocampo on the highlands to the south are laid out in a grid with a central square and streets extending out in neat parallel rows. By contrast, one reached the houses of the Nahuat in Huitzilan by walking up narrow meandering paths along ridges and arroyos. Those of the mestizos tended to line the main street just west of the stream that flows along the valley floor.

Nacho's ancestral home was nestled in Calyecapan, which means "Place of the Last House" in the community and refers to a locality just below the ridge forming the northern boundary of the Huitzilan valley. From that ridge, a visitor could look south and see the houses of the entire village laid out on the valley floor and extending up along another ridge rising toward the "Man of Stone Mountain," or Tacalot, in the east. Halfway up that ridge was the cattle pasture of Talcuaco, visible from everywhere in the valley. The observer from Calyecapan could see the domed church at the midpoint on the valley floor, and the old school building with its magnificently high porch facing the church on the other side of the street. The large white masonry homes with red tile roofs of the first mestizo settlers clustered on both sides of the main street just

Huitzilan and Cihuatepet from Calyecapan

south of the church. Those of more recent mestizo settlers lined the eastern side of the main street halfway between the church and Calyecapan.

The Nahuat of Huitzilan, like the Nahuas in other parts of Mexico,[3] are oriented very precisely to named localities organized mentally according to the four cardinal directions. The Nahuat assign a gender to the mountains flanking Huitzilan to east and west in accord with the movement of the masculine sun. The mountains to the east are masculine because the sun rises behind "Man of Stone Mountain," or Tacalot, and those to the west are feminine because the sun sets behind "Woman Mountain," or Cihuatepet. Some Nahuat say men will die if there is a landslide on the eastern mountains and women will die if there is one on the western mountains. In between are many localities that make up the town of Huitzilan, including a place called Talcez, or "Leg of Land," where Nacho lived with Victoria. Talcez is halfway between the domed church in the center of town and Calyecapan, where Nacho was born and lived his childhood and early adult years prior to marrying Victoria.

In March of 2004, I walked, as I had on many occasions, to Nacho's house in Talcez with my tape recorder packed in my cloth bag, entered

Victoria, Nacho, and first Adrian

his courtyard, and called out his name. After a moment's hesitation, he showed that he had recognized my voice and replied with "Jaime. Come inside." Ducking to avoid the low beam over the doorway, I entered his darkened house, where he shook my hand and then offered me the worn-out wicker chair. He sat down on his bed in front of me, and I pulled my tape recorder out of my cloth bag, untangled the cord, and handed him the microphone. He was silent for a moment as he composed his thoughts for what he was going to say. We had decided earlier that he would talk about his life with Victoria. They had started their courtship in 1970, two years after I arrived in their community. He was working with me by then as well as with the priest, who took Nacho and two other Nahuat men around on his visits to other churches in his parish. Nacho learned to give catechism classes and lead prayers in family rituals and came into the main church of Huitzilan often. He spoke clearly into the microphone, and, with a note of sadness, he told how his courtship with Victoria started in the church and then turned into a good marriage: "And since we went into the church a lot, we got a craving for each other. I and my wife, Victoria. We had fallen in love and we thought about it, and it had been a year. We took a year to think about getting married. We lived together. We were happy. We were doing so well, but then the bad thing happened."

For Nacho, the bad thing started when the UCI leaders from Veracruz held their first meeting in 1977 in Huitzilan. "According to them, they came to divide up the land, to help the poor. A lot of people went to the meeting. They thought the UCI would really help them. They got bold after the meeting and asked around about excess land. There was a man who wanted to stand up and look for land that's called 'intestate,' where whoever has it now does not have papers. The person who didn't have papers was not going to work that land, and so they could take it. At first the UCI didn't do anything. But afterwards they started fighting our brothers. They worked Talcuaco. They planted corn and they probably intended to divide it up among the men who worked it, according to what they contributed to the crop. And they also planted here by the cemetery in Taltempan, where the school is now. They also planted there. So then they went after that one they call Wolf." Wolf was a Nahuat who aligned himself with the mestizo who allegedly ordered the destruction of the Talcuaco cornfield. Nacho and I chose the pseudonym Wolf for this Nahuat man because he had a reputation for wanting women who were in relationships with other men and using violence to get them. Nacho continued: "They say the UCIs really went after Wolf. And that went on for days, and they couldn't do anything to him. He fled. He helped himself. Until the day came when they fought. There was a big lad named Ramirez, Wolf's half brother. They put a bullet in him. But they didn't wound him badly, and he fled. He found his brother Wolf. Ramirez and Wolf were brothers. So then Wolf and Ramirez attacked the UCIs. They attacked Felipe Reyes."

Felipe Reyes was one of the UCI leaders who allegedly came from Veracruz. "Felipe Reyes" is also the name of a Robin Hood character in a popular radio drama broadcast over XEW at the time the UCI arrived in Huitzilan.

Nacho resumed: "Well, they shot Felipe Reyes. So then, yes, the UCIs retreated. Some had remained in town. Then they started working again, those who had fled. Afterwards they got bolder. Afterwards, they came back. But the rich ones, Coyote's family, and the president, a Nahuat who went in with him, they brought the *federales*, the soldiers, to go after the UCIs." Nacho and I chose the pseudonym Coyote for the mestizo who made a dubious claim that he had rights of ownership in the Talcuaco cattle pasture and tried to drive the UCI out of Huitzilan. Coyote was greedy for land much as the "Coyote" character in the popular trickster tale in Huitzilan, "Rabbit and Coyote," was greedy for turkey and chicken meat. Nacho continued: "There were many *federales* who pursued the UCI. Until one day, they broke up the milpa the UCI had planted. They cut down the entire milpa. That's when the rage [cuala-yot] began. The UCI started killing. They became blind with rage. They started spying. They spied. Until they just killed even if their victims did not have fault. They killed secretly [they shot their victims in the back]."

Nacho and Victoria

Nacho and Victoria were caught in the middle of this conflict because Nacho served as justice of the peace in the town hall government from February 1979 to the end of 1981. He was included in the list of those some in the UCI suspected were against them because the town hall president had allegedly sided with Coyote in the dispute over Talcuaco. However, Victoria's father and brothers were members of the UCI. Nacho explained that his father-in-law said that the UCI persuaded him to join by offering to protect him from authorities who intended to punish him for killing his daughter Clemencia's suitor. Officials of the town hall ordinarily serve three-year terms, and those who began their terms on February 15, 1979, were all on a slate of candidates nominated by a local Partido Revolucionario Institucional (PRI) committee. Coyote's nephew, a man we call Rake, because he reputedly fathered sixty children with Nahuat women, was on the slate as the town hall president scheduled to enter that February, and he had told Nacho he would be the next justice of the peace. The justice of the peace is a minor official who deals with petty crimes and disputes involving small amounts of money (under twenty-five pesos in 1979). Between 1968 and 1978, it was customary to have a Nahuat as justice of the peace, and Nacho's older brother, Miguel, had served in this office during that period. Justices of the peace in Huitzilan have to deal with family quarrels Nahuat men and women bring to the town hall. Those quarrels sometimes involve disputes between a mother and daughter-in-law, which, although serious from the perspective of the members of a family, are really not punishable offenses. It is to the advantage of many in the community to have a respected Nahuat who understands the culture adjudicating such disputes.

Nacho felt he had no choice but to enter the town hall government, and he reconstructed the conversation with Rake in the following way:

Rake: "You're coming in here."

Nacho: "But I can't."

Rake: "You're coming in here."

Nacho described what happened after he and Rake took office on the fifteenth of February: "The president, Rake, had his policemen. It was this way. The UCIs started to kill the town hall policemen, they killed them. Until the policemen fled. Those they could not kill, fled. So then it went on until Rake resigned from office, and that man, the Nahuat who worked with Coyote, went in. Well the town hall policemen got stronger. The police went back in. They organized another band of policemen. The UCIs were arrested. They arrested the UCIs. Until the day came when they spied on the president. They killed him. The policemen fled. The police fled. So then we continued as justice of the peace and civil justice. I was still justice of the peace. Until another Nahuat went in. He was president. First he had worked as Agente de Ministerio Público [who handles more serious cases than those referred to either one of the justices]. And he didn't last long after becoming president. He didn't last. They killed him." Regarding his last days in the town hall, Nacho said: "Just me and Gonzalo Martínez, the civil justice, with whom I worked, were left. We worked together until I left at the end of 1981. The UCI were always after us. We went through a very dangerous period, and it was so bad, so awful, that I couldn't leave the house. I couldn't even get wood. I couldn't go anywhere."

Nacho described how he discovered he was on the list of those some in the UCI wanted to murder. "Many people, who were good people, came to see me. One man said, 'Be careful because those people are after you.'" I asked Nacho who helped him in those days, and he said his father-in-law. "He helped us so that we had something to eat. He helped us." Nacho explained: "My brothers-in-law weren't good men, because they wanted to lure me into a trap. They wanted me to walk around.

"Brothers-n-law: 'Walk around, walk around. Go to the milpa where you usually go. The UCIs won't do anything to you. We talked among ourselves.'

"And we told my father-in-law, who said:

"'It's not true. Don't believe them just because these guys say they won't shoot you. When they see you, they'll shoot you. Don't go anywhere.'"

Nacho experienced several threats to his life, which confirmed what he learned from his father-in-law and others, that it was dangerous for him in Huitzilan.

Nacho's Father-in-law

A crucial piece of Nacho's story is the role his father-in-law played in protecting him from other members of the UCI, including from his own sons. The story of his father-in-law's involvement with the UCI goes back several years before the invasion of the Talcuaco and Taltempan cattle pastures. Once when visiting Nacho and Victoria in their Talcez home around 1975, I found Victoria very animated and alarmed as she told Nacho about a fight that broke out between her father and a boy who was courting her older sister, Clemencia. Victoria was telling Nacho that Clemencia's suitor had made her drop the bucket of boiled corn she was taking to the mill to grind for the morning meal. Apparently he had confronted her and perhaps tried to force her to have sex. Victoria's father, Juan, quarreled with the boy and eventually shot and killed him when they confronted each other again. These events took place just before the arrival of the UCI in Huitzilan in 1977 and are important in several respects for understanding Nacho and Victoria's marriage and what happened after the army chopped down the Talcuaco milpa. They reveal how Victoria's father disapproved of and was willing to confront and fight any man who treated his daughters with disrespect. The UCI apparently used the history of this conflict to obligate Victoria's father to join in the invasion of the Talcuaco pasture. Once in the UCI, Victoria's father protected Nacho from being killed by the group for having served in the town hall government as justice of the peace between 1979 and 1981. Victoria's father's contrasting relationships with two men who courted his daughters—Nacho and Clemencia's suitor—are further support for the conclusion that Victoria and Nacho had a marriage with respect. Had Nacho disrespected Victoria, then he would not have benefited from his father-in-law's protection during a very tense period in Huitzilan's history.

Nacho recalled the quarrel between his father-in-law and Clemencia's suitor in 2004, and his recollection accords very closely with my field notes. He said: "Well, the boy asked to marry Clemencia. He asked for the girl. But the boy did a disrespectful thing. He wanted her where he saw her. One time he decided to grab her when the girl was going to the corn mill. And he made her spill the nextamal [corn boiled in lime for making tortillas]. That's why they quarreled. Then one time my father-in-law went to work in his milpa and ran into that boy. And they say they fought. The boy started hitting my father-in-law in the head with his machete. So then my father-in-law helped himself, but he came home very badly wounded. So then he got better. When he ran into him again, that's when he carried a gun and he shot him." Nacho explained how the UCIs used this past history to persuade his father-in-law to join their group. "He wasn't working with the UCI. He wasn't working with them. He went into the group because the UCIs frightened him. One of the UCIs said, 'Well, for you to be free, come in with us.' So then he joined them. Then they didn't do anything to him. He went in with them."

The First Encounter with Wrath

Nacho's father-in-law played an important but indirect role in saving him from Wrath, who was one of the Nahuat leaders of the UCI. Wrath is a pseudonym we chose for a man who had married and separated from Wolf's sister. He was among the contingent of Nahuat who invited the UCI leader from Veracruz, Felipe Reyes, to come to Huitzilan to help them deal with Wolf. Nacho described the first time that Wrath came to the church to kill him and how Victoria saved Nacho from Wrath by invoking the name of her father.

One time I was in church. I was teaching some small children catechism. The children were there, and I showed them some little dolls. One day Wrath went in. He went over to watch me.

Wrath: "Let the children pray first and then us."

Nacho: "Fine."

Wrath: "How come you sit in front, and I don't like that."

Nacho: "No, I put myself next to them." They drew nearer. "I put myself here."

He reached over and grabbed my arm with his hand. He grabbed me like this. [Nacho showed me how Wrath grabbed his forearm and squeezed it in a viselike grip.] He grabbed me hard.

Wrath: "Now you're in my grasp. Now you're in my grasp. You act big now."

Nacho: "I don't act big. I want it this way because the children know me."

We worked together on my milpa. That man worked with us. I said, "I'm not acting big."

Wrath: "Where do you have your guns? It seems you're hiding guns. A firearm."

Nacho: "I don't have a gun. I never carry a gun."

Wrath: "Do you remember when you shot at us? Tell us where the guns are."

Nacho: "I don't know anything about that. I never took a gun. Only the agente has them or the presidente. But they didn't give any of those guns to me."

Wrath: "But you're still in my grasp. And I can't do anything here while these children are all around us. Let's go outside."

He dragged me along with his hand. Then I was outside, it was drizzling now, and my son Alfonso, he was a little child, perhaps like this child [pointing to his grandson Brian], and he drew near me. The children rose up. Many of them went to find me again. And my wife, Alfonso's mother, she went to find us. Wrath had taken me outside.

Wrath: "We can't be here. Let's go outside."

He took me to the base of the church tower. And he took me there by force. I was in his grasp, and he had his pistol here [pointing to the right side of his waist]. Instead of grabbing his gun with his right hand, he grabbed me. And he couldn't grab his gun with his left hand.

Wrath: "I have you in my grasp here."

His eyes were like those of a rabid dog. They were all red. He was licking his lips. He was terrifying.

Wrath: "I have you in my grasp."

One of my nephews was there, and he saw Wrath pass by. Wrath was giving me orders.

Nephew: "Let go of my uncle. He's not a disrespectful person."

Wrath: "You'll be a captive, if you don't get out of here."

Then my wife also went there. Then she started to scold Wrath. She started to restrain him.

Victoria: "Let go of my husband because he isn't doing anything to you. Calm down."

He didn't calm down.

Victoria: "I know what is going on here because I know my husband. You know my house where I live. You've also seen my father there. You'll deal with my father, not with him."

He let me go. I was there for a long time until the man calmed down enough to let me go.

Wrath: "We'll talk again."

He let me go and left.

The Second Encounter with Wrath

Confrontations continued between Nahuat in the UCI and other Nahuat, as Nacho revealed when he described a second encounter with Wrath, who came to kill Nacho again in the church. This encounter with Wrath led Nacho and Victoria to conclude that he could no longer go to his milpa and had to leave the community to earn money to feed their children. The encounter took place when Nacho went to church, this time to pray. In his account of what happened, Nacho mentions the church in the center of town, the basketball court to the west of the church, his escape through a dark passageway that leads to the basketball court, and the old school and the town hall, both of which are lined up across the street and to the west of the church on slightly higher ground. Nacho was kneeling at the altar with his son Alfonso when he heard Wrath and Dog's son approach on the basketball court. Nacho and I chose the pseudonym Dog for a second local Nahuat leader in the UCI who joined Wrath in the contingent of men who brought Felipe Reyes to Huitzilan to deal with Wolf. We chose Dog for this man because, from the Nahuat point of view, he was promiscuous like a dog. He was married to one woman and was in a relationship with a second one who was also the object of Wolf's desire. Just as Wrath and Dog came into the church, Nacho and his son escaped through the dark passage and ran past the town hall, down through the shallow arroyo and toward his house in Talcez. Wrath left the church when he couldn't find Nacho and went up to the porch in front of the old school to spot where he had gone.

Here is Nacho's description of these events:

We went on and we went on until I could no longer leave the house. I couldn't do it anymore. It was because they were spying on me. One time my wife said, "I'm going to my mother's house."

Nacho: "Fine."

Victoria: "Are you going to the church?"

Nacho: "I don't know if I'll go."

But my Alfonso said, "Let's go to the church, papá. Let's go to the church."

Nacho: "I can't go because I sense someone will be there."

Alfonso: "Let's go to the church."

Nacho: "I don't know."

It turned out the boy convinced me.

Nacho: "Let's go."

I always told my wife, I said to her: "I'm going. When I go to the church, you come meet me."

Victoria: "Fine."

Because I'd go, only if my wife accompanied me. I couldn't go if she didn't. Those people spied on me. So then from there, it turned out that I listened to my boy. I found a reason to go. I went to the church. I went and knelt on a prayer bench. And my boy was playing outside. He was in front of the church. That's when Wrath came onto the basketball court next to the church. And he carried a pistol in his waistband, and he was with a man. He was with Dog's son. Those two were together. They came closer. Wrath spoke, he was talking to Dog's son, and he asked him, "What did you bring?"

Dog's son: "I brought a gun, but it's a small one. It's not big."

Nacho: "Híjole."

And that's when I felt him running up in back of me. Híjole. I felt terrible. Híjole. It was as if I were lost. I felt awful.

Then I thought, I told my boy [who had joined Nacho in front of the altar], "Get up."

Alfonso: "Where are we going?"

Nacho: "Get up. Quietly. Get up. Let's go out through this small door."

Then the boy got up, and I left one of my small books I had brought. I got up and went out the door. I passed through that dark passage to the outside. I jumped over a wall. There were a lot of rocks at that time. I climbed over them.

Nacho and his son Alfonso started running up the main street of Huitzilan. They headed north past the town hall and toward their home. Periodically, Nacho asked Alfonso if Wrath and Dog's son were pursuing them.

Nacho: "Run. And turn around to see if he comes."

So my boy turned around quickly.

Alfonso: "He isn't coming. We've come a long way quickly."

Nacho: "They won't come. If they do come, they won't do anything to us. They won't shoot us. We've escaped. If they come, we'll run."

And we arrived at the house. We were inside.

Nacho: "I won't go there again. You know what'll happen if I go somewhere."

After we made it home, I had been there maybe ten minutes when my niece showed up, Jovita from Calyecapan.

Jovita: "You're here?"

Nacho: "Yes."

Jovita: "Híjole. You left the house. And those men chased after you right away. Wrath came out onto the porch [of the school across the street from the church]. He stood on the porch up above while other UCI were walking around the church below looking high and low for where you were."

Nacho: "We came right back here."

So then I couldn't leave the house. To fetch firewood or anything. I came to the point where I was in very, very bad shape. I suffered greatly. . . . From that point on, I was never free. They held me down while they pursued me. That's why I couldn't leave the house. And I went on like that, I went on, I went on. Because they didn't lack someone to hold down, someone to hunt. Until the day came when they spied on those who were their enemies or on someone with whom they were angry. They spied on him and killed him. They killed him. But others remained. Even though I walked to the center of town, I wasn't free. I wasn't free even to work or to earn money or to bring firewood. I don't know how I survived. We suffered a lot. We suffered a lot. That's the way it was as we suffered more. It got worse for us. Híjole. Until the day came when my wife said, "Go work up above. Go look for work. Go to Mexico City to see what you can do so these children can eat."

Nacho: "Right."

Nacho explained: "While my father-in-law was alive, I went along fine going to Mexico City. I'd stay a month. I'd come home. I brought money. Then I wouldn't go. I'd go again. I wouldn't stay long. One month, a month and a half. I'd come back again because they needed money here."

Nacho worked in construction when in Mexico City.

Victoria's Death

The violence reached a new turn when the Antorcha Campesina appeared in the village in 1983. The Antorcha Campesina is an organization, affiliated with the PRI, that took over the town hall of Huitzilan in March of 1984 and held power up to and including the year 2004, when Nacho told his story of love and loss. One of those who probably fell to an Antorcha bullet in one of the first battles was Nacho's father-in-law. Nacho and Victoria were in a very dangerous position following his father-in-law's death because they had lost the one man who had shielded them from those in the UCI who wanted to kill Nacho for serving as justice of the peace in the town hall government. With the death of his father-in-law, Nacho felt he had to leave Huitzilan and join many from his village who sought refuge from the UCI by living in Zacapoaxtla, a commercial center on the highlands thirty-two kilometers from Huitzilan. Nacho had found a job working in a bakery and had been in Zacapoaxtla for just a few days when he heard that Victoria had died. On the day she died,

Nacho thought he had heard a horse outside the door of the house where he slept—an extremely bad omen to the Nahuat, having possible antecedents in the Conquest, when Spaniards rode horses in battle against the ancient Aztecs. Many mestizos, but no Nahuat, rode horses in Huitzilan in the days when mestizos rode them around the interior of the sierra, before the construction of roads in the early 1970s.

Nacho described how he heard the news.

I had just been there one week. I went on the fourth of October, and in that same month on the fifteenth of October they killed my wife and all of her family. I was in Zacapoaxtla. I learned the terrible news. I did not know they had killed her at the moment of her death. I did not know it. Only at that time, on the fifteenth when we went to bed, I heard something but I didn't know what it was. We heard it outside the door. Do you remember how a horse shakes itself? It jingles. Its bridle jingles, and it snorts loudly. That's what I heard. I even went out but I didn't see anything. Well, fine. It was on a Tuesday I went to the plaza. We had finished where we were working, we were working in a bakery, we had finished, and I went to the plaza. And Sebastiana Arellano and Polo went to find me. Did you know Polo? They told me. That's where Sebastiana said, "Nacho, I'm going to warn you."

I said, "What?"

"Forgive me for telling you something so big you can't imagine it. Your wife, they killed her. She was buried on Tuesday."

Nacho recalled his reaction to hearing the news of Victoria's death from Sebastiana Arellano.

I felt terrible. What could I do? Nothing. Nothing. I felt so bad, I felt lost where I was. Híjole. I felt terrible. I felt terrible. So then I arrived at my patrón's house. I told my patrón what happened to me.

Nacho: "They took my wife from me. They shot my wife."

Patrón: "Híjole."

They gave me a tea.

Patrón: "Drink this tea. I give it to you so you won't get sick."

Nacho recalled asking Sebastiana Arellano about his children, "And my children?"

Sebastiana: "Your children are fine. Nothing happened to them."

Nacho: "And Cinorina?"

Sebastiana: "She hurt her forehead here [pointing]. She caught it on a piece of barbed wire when she and her grandmother fled."

They fled when those men from the UCI arrived. And my other son, he's Juanito now, he was just three months old. And there he was where his mother had fallen. The child was in her shadow. He was screaming. How he suffered there, and he was an infant!

Nacho Learns about the Wounded

Nacho described what happened to his mother-in-law, Angelina, her daughter Berta, and his daughter Cinorina. All three escaped, but not without injury.

They fled when those men of the UCI arrived. My mother-in-law, Angelina, had to flee. One of her daughters, Berta, they also shot her. They also got to her. They shot her here [gesturing to between her thighs]. Here. She got hit on both of her legs. She was a little hurt, but she's all right. And my mother-in-law, Angelina, also got hit here [gesturing to the stomach]. They removed shotgun pellets from her stomach. She fled with my child, with Cinorina. That's when Cinorina got caught on the wire here on her forehead. Here [gesturing].

Sebastiana: "She got cut on her forehead, just a little, but she did not have any more wounds. There's nothing you can do. Don't think anything crazy. Don't go to Huitzilan. Don't go so they'll shoot you. Your children are fine. Your children are at your brother's. Only the little one, Juanito, he's with Adela [a mestiza]. She has him down there by Manuel Mina's place. They're taking care of him."

Nacho: "Good."

Polo: "Don't go. Don't go. Those people in the UCI won't leave you alone."

Nacho came up with his own understanding of the events that led to the massacre, which he attributed to a quarrel that developed within the UCI over the gun his father-in-law had used to kill Clemencia's disrespectful suitor. He began by describing Clemencia and Eugenia as hotheads, or "tahuel cihuameh," a term that many Nahuat used to describe the women in their families. Clemencia and Eugenia were angry over the death of their brother, also called "Nacho," who died when his companions killed him for his father's famous gun.

Well, first of all, my sisters-in-law were hotheads. Did you know Clemencia and Eugenia? Florentino? They were all hotheads. The UCIs killed my brother-in-law "Nacho." His same companions! And "Nacho" carried a gun that belonged to his father. But they got drunk together, and they took the gun from him after they killed him. That's how it was. Then these sisters-in-law, they were very fierce, they went to tell those men something strong like this:

"You killed 'Nacho.' Just as you killed him, so you'll die."

My sisters-in-law were angry because those UCIs had killed their brother. So then the killers got angry about what Clemencia and Eugenia had said to them. For that reason, the day came when the killers went to my mother-in-law's house and killed my sisters-in-law.

After Victoria

Nacho turned to his children to rebuild his life after Victoria died in the massacre of 1983. Victoria left five children, whose names and birth dates are as follows: Epifania (1974), Alfonso (1975), Cinorina (1978), Adrian (1980), and Juanito (1983). Her firstborn was also named Adrian (1971), but he died, as did many infant children in Huitzilan. I saw Nacho lavish affection on the first Adrian and speak to him in Nahuat baby talk, a practice he continues with his grandchildren. He called him "papá" and played with the infant on the bed.

Like many Nahuat from Huitzilan, Nacho could not return to his community without risking his own life, and so he found a way to get his children out of the village and take them to Zacapoaxtla, where they spent five months in exile. He described their life in exile, beginning with how he reunited with his children in Zapotitlán, the next town to the north of Huitzilan. In his description, he mentioned running into the army that had gone into the sierra to back up the Antorcha in driving the UCI out of Huitzilan. Nacho's account reveals that the UCI faced a highly organized force bent on its annihilation. Nacho made his trip to Zapotitlán within a week or two of Victoria's death, and so he must have run into the army sometime around the end of October. Here is what he said:

In the meantime, I looked and looked for a way to see my children. I asked around for anyone who came from Zapotitlán. Then I found Facundo from here. I asked him, "When will you go to Zapotitlán? When will you go to Zapotitlán?"

Facundo: "Well, I'll go in another week. Why?"

Nacho: "I want to go with you because I want to see my children. Let's go to Zapotitlán."

Facundo: "Fine."

The day came.

Facundo: "We're going early in the morning."

Nacho: "Fine. Then I'll go with you."

Facundo: "Fine."

Then we came. We arrived in Zapotitlán. And there were soldiers. So then I went to see them.

Nacho: "Help me. I'd like a favor."

Soldier: "What?"

Nacho: "I'm looking for the lieutenant."

Soldier: "He isn't here. He's in Huitzilan."

Nacho: "That's where I have my children and I want to bring them. Because they say, I don't know if it's true, some people say, if someone shoots one of you, you'll bomb the town."

Soldier: "No. Yes, if they shoot one of us, or shoot at us, or it appears they might shoot us. That's when many soldiers will go look for all those people, they'll grab them. They'll shoot them. Children. They won't do anything to them. Women. They won't do anything to them. They don't need to worry about us. Yes, the big, the big ones. Yes, they'll seize them, but children, no. So then it won't be that way. Come in a while, and the lieutenant will tell us. If he says we're to bring your children, we'll go bring them to you."

Nacho: "Good."

Then I waited there. I waited. I walked around. And Choni arrived. She's Rosa's daughter, she went to Zapotitlán to shop in the CONASUPO [government-run grocery store]. There weren't any stores in Huitzilan anymore. They were closed. She went to Zapotitlán to get sugar, beans, what she could not get in Huitzilan. So then I asked her, I said, "Please tell my sisters-in-law that I'm here. Bring my children."

Then I didn't see that soldier again. I waited for my children. Then the next day, my sisters-in-law brought me my children. Little Adrian, he was just a small child three years old. Well, right away he went over to me and he wanted to talk to me. But he couldn't talk. Then I hugged him, and we spent one night in the house of my compadre, Benjamin Vazquez. We slept there. I wanted us to stay there, but my children didn't want to. They said no because they feared that perhaps those men would find them there, perhaps the UCIs would find them. They didn't want me to stay there. We slept there one night, and the next day my mother-in-law arrived, my mother-in-law, Angelina. She brought her daughter, who was wounded here [between her thighs], and Angelina was hurt too. She arrived at the priest's house. The priest told me to take her to see a doctor. We went to where Dr. Fausto was. We took her. He saw how bad the girl was.

Dr. Fausto: "Take her to Zacapoaxtla. I can't cure her."

The next day we went to Zacapoaxtla. We took all of the children. I asked to go back in where I was before. Again we looked for a way to eat. We stayed there a long time. We lived with one of my sisters-in-law. My mother-in-law stayed in the clinic in Zacapoaxtla. There by the Seguro Social. She went there. But we just lived on. We slept [with my sister-in-law]. Meanwhile, I asked for my old job back. I began again to ask about work. They gave [the job] back to me. And I rented a house. I started renting, and I worked. I was working but I wasn't doing well because I was earning very little. I earned one and a half pesos a day. That was very little. It was not good at all.

Return

The time was March 1984, the Antorcha Campesina had taken over the town hall in Huitzilan, and Nacho brought his children back to the village. He described the suffering of his family and of himself while living in exile in Zacapoaxtla and then returning to Huitzilan to put his home and his life back together. He represented the precarious state of his family by describing how his son Adrian became very sick after returning to Huitzilan. Nacho told how he had to care for his children, healing their illness, combing their hair, bathing them, washing their clothes, and grinding the corn dough for their tortillas. He did embroidery, a skill he had learned from Victoria, to support his family.

We suffered hardship until the day came when Carlos, who was in Zacapoaxtla, said, "Let's go home. If you'll go, I'll go. Go with me."

Nacho: "Yes. If you'll go, let's go."

Then we took my children.

Nacho to his children: "You're going home. Some from here are going back."

Children: "Well let's go. We'll go too. Where you go, we'll go."

They didn't want to stay in Zacapoaxtla anymore. We all came. We came that day. I don't remember if it was on the twenty-first of March, but it was around that date. We came back. We spent the night in the town hall. From there we went to where my brothers are. I stayed there for a long time. I got tired of being where older brother Miguel is. I went to where middle brother Colax is. I also got tired of being there. My Adrian started to get sick. And a woman I knew said to him, "You're very sick." Turning to me she said, "I don't know if he'll get well."

She couldn't do anything. So then I came home. I swept everything, and I fixed it up a little. I told the children, "It's better to go home now."

Everything was all strewn around in the front as if I had fought in a battle. It was awful. Then I swept. And I bought some beans, sugar. It seems I had corn. I put the electric wire back into the house. It was lying all over the ground. The wire wasn't cut. There was juice. My neighbor Cresencio was a good man. He paid for the electricity. Afterwards I paid him for it. From there, we came just as we were. I brought the children here. I started treating Adrian. Women gave me some advice. One of them had this medicine, and she gave it to me. I gave it to him and started to bathe him. So he'd get better. I continued until the boy was fine. He was fine. I suffered greatly with him. Adrian was only three years old. Cinorina was about six years old. And Alfonso was eight years old. And Epifania was nine years old. They were all small children. I ground tortilla dough for them. I combed their hair. I washed their clothes. I bathed them. I did it but it was a lot. I suffered a lot to the point I couldn't do it. Until they were older, Epifania was about thirteen, she was big. I said to her, "Now you can bathe yourself. You can wash your own clothes. Wash them yourself now. You can do it for them. Wash your brothers' clothes. If not, I'll wash them."

So then that's what she did. We realized they were getting big already. Epifania could grind tortilla dough herself. But while she was in school, I ground tortilla dough for them, I washed their clothes, and they went to school. That's how we lived, but I suffered a lot of hardships.

Epifania Grieves Her Mother

For Nacho's children, Victoria's death was a personal tragedy. Epifania, Nacho and Victoria's oldest child, recalled what her mother's death meant and continues to mean for her.

I wanted to see my mother. I was crying. We were crying because we wanted to go see her but how could we? Grandmother said she was dead. They had shot her. After they buried my mother, we went to sleep down at my other grandmother's, where my grandfather Ponciano lived [Talteno]. We went there to sleep. Then we went up where my uncles are [Calyecapan]. They took us there to sleep. Yes, because my father wasn't here. He was in Zacapoaxtla. That's where he was. He couldn't come here, and so we were in Calyecapan. And then he came to Zapotitlán, and they took us there at nightfall. They took

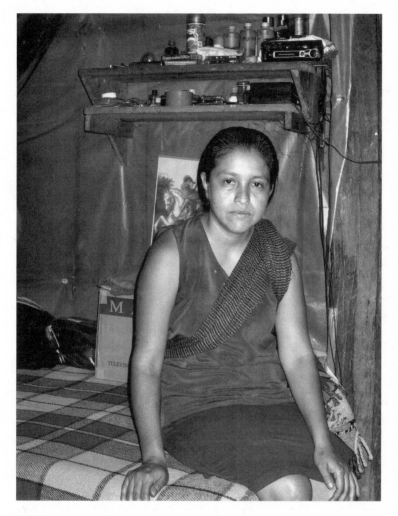

Epifania

us because he wanted to see us, and he couldn't come here. So then my aunts and cousins dropped us off in Zapotitlán. Yes. There I was. And after we spent I don't know how many days there, they took us to Zacapoaxtla [a market town thirty-two kilometers from Huitzilan]. We went there to stay. They took us there. I don't know how many months we were there, but, yes, we stayed a long time. We were very hungry. We suffered a lot because there was no one to take care of us, and my father was working. There was no one to give us a tortilla because my grandmother was in the hospital. They had shot her too. So then my father took care of us, but we suffered a lot. Then we came back here, but not until we saw that others, who had left Huitzilan, were returning. They could not be in Huitzilan, because the UCIs wanted to shoot them. So they had fled. And then came the organization that's here now [the Antorcha]. Then we heard that they were bringing the people back. We told my father to bring us back too. We also wanted to return. And that's how it was. And we waited until they brought us back. We spent another, I don't know, perhaps a month up there where my uncles are [Calyecapan]. That's where we were after we arrived here. We didn't come here [Talcez], because they had stolen things from my father. We couldn't come right back in here until my father put things in order. Everything was scattered around. They took all of the adobes that were here. The beams, the same thing. They took all of them. It was a battle scene all over.

Well, I couldn't do anything. My brothers and sister were small children. I couldn't even grind tortilla dough. My father ground tortilla dough for us and he bathed us. My mother would not let us do anything. We suffered the day she was lost. And then my father took care of us.

I was very sad, and I cried because I wanted to see my mother. My brothers and sister did too. They looked for my mother. We were sad and we cried. What could we do? We didn't see her anymore. We suffered a lot. We were cold and hungry in Zacapoaxtla. That's how it was, but we survived.

We didn't fully realize what had happened, because we were children. We were sad then but not as much as later. When we were older, ten or twelve, we felt it more and we were sadder. But where could I find her, and she wasn't alive? I looked for her a lot because my mother loved me. If sometimes we were bad and someone wanted to hit me, then my mother talked to him so he wouldn't hit me. Yes. That's what I remember. That's the way it was until I got big.

Nacho Remarries

Nacho continued his story by explaining why he decided to look for another woman to help him with the work of raising his small children so he could earn some money.

I suffered a lot until I had spent three years raising them myself when I found another woman. And I thought, "Well, I'm going to look for a woman because I won't last. I can't work. I can't go anywhere. I have my children to watch."

I did embroidery. I'd finish it, and I gave it all to Sebastiana Arellano. I sold her a lot of it. She took it all from here, and that's how we got along in a middling way. That's how I got along in a middling way.

Then I looked for a wife. Then Manuela was with me. She was happy here with her daughters. We were good. She was Gabi's daughter. It was good with her. We were doing fine. She was very good. She wasn't sickly. She was strong. She was good. But we saw the day here when work got to a point. If we planted coffee now, well, there would be money. There would be money after we helped cut coffee, but come June we were left with nothing. There wasn't any money. It ended. I did not know how I could plant. I was not very free. I was not free to work, because those people were around so much. The UCIs. I wasn't free. I couldn't go wherever I wanted then. So Manuela said one day, "Go to Mexico City and work. Go work in Mexico City. Spend two or three weeks and come back, and bring money for these children to eat."

Nacho: "I don't know. Perhaps something will happen to you."

Because I felt that something bad would happen to them.

Manuela: "Nothing will happen to us. Your children are all right. The children were sick and now they're fine. They are good. Nothing will happen to them. Don't worry."

Nacho: "Well, good."

I walked. I went into a construction project where they built houses. I worked for about two weeks—not two weeks, one week—and it was on the third day of the next week, after I had left Huitzilan, when someone called me on the telephone. They sent for me around nine o'clock at night. They came over to talk to me.

Person on the telephone: "They looked for you because they took your wife."

I thought perhaps they ran off with her, perhaps they kidnapped her.

Person on the telephone: "The woman got sick and died."

Nacho: "Why?"

Person on the telephone: "I don't know why. But you're not going to get sick. Be strong. Go see your children. You're going to see your children. Don't be afraid. Don't do anything wild. Don't be unreliable [don't fall apart]."

Nacho: "No. No. What would I do?"

And there was a lad named Luis. Perhaps you know Juana's boy, Luis? He worked with me.

Luis: "Well, I'll go with you. Don't worry. I'll help."

Nacho: "Well, good."

Then we came. We came from Mexico City. Then we arrived near here, and my daughter went to find me. My little girl, who is big already, she was two. She had suffered tremendously. I suffered tremendously. Then I said, "This won't cost me." That is, it was not so difficult for me to care for the girl, because her sisters and brothers were very big already. Epifania, well she was big already. Cinorina also. So then Epifania or Cinorina began to bathe her, to wash her clothes. Well, it wasn't difficult for her to grow up. But right then she suffered, she suffered until now when she stopped suffering. But I suffered after I had been complete. The heartache hurt me too. That heartache really finished me because I don't know how I did it. Something grabbed me, it wasn't a big sickness, because it did not finish me, but I felt that I would not get well. Until now, though I'm fine, I'm well now, but I always remember.

Nacho Today

Nacho finds himself today in the same position as his mother when I met them both in 1968. She was a widow then, and he is a widower now, and both were or are the heads of extended family households. Like his mother then, Nacho lives now with his two married sons, their wives, and their children. In small but important ways Nacho reminds me of his mother in how he is with his children and his daughters-in-law. His mother encouraged him to continue attending school after his father's death, and, like his mother, he encouraged Epifania and the others to go to school after Victoria's death. Also like his mother, Nacho treats his daughters-in-law with respect. One small example occurred when I visited Nacho in his home. Most Nahuat would offer a visitor a cup of coffee and perhaps even a meal if they held their guest in particularly high regard. Ordinarily, women cook and manage the kitchen in a Nahuat household, although Nacho explained that he worked in the kitchen to feed his small children after returning to Huitzilan. Unlike what one might find in another domestic group, Nacho never asks his daughters-in-law to serve me a cup of coffee. Nacho gets up, serves the coffee from the pot sitting on the hearth, and gives the cup to me himself. He had described how his mother also treated her daughters-in-law with respect despite her reputation for being a tahuel cihuat, or hotheaded woman.

Nacho's two married sons, who currently live in his household, are Alfonso, named after Alfonso Angel, Nacho's father, and Adrian, which is also Nacho's legal name. Earlier, Nacho had described meeting Adrian, then only three, in Zapotitlán shortly after Victoria's death. Nacho told how the boy tried to talk to him but could not speak because he was traumatized by what had happened to his mother. Nacho also told how

Alfonso, Josefina, and Victor Alfonso

Adrian became very ill shortly after returning to Huitzilan in March of 1984. Adrian married Esperanza, and they have a son, Brian. Alfonso married Josefina, and they have two children, Victor Alfonso, named after Victoria and Nacho's father, Alfonso, and Yocelyn. Epifania lives with her husband in another part of Huitzilan, and they have two children, one of whom is a daughter named Victoria.

Some things are different from how they were when Nacho was a young man earning a half a measure of corn for a full day of work. Now he raises the corn that fills his granary by sharecropping his small plot of land on the other side of the mountains flanking Huitzilan to the east. As the landowner, he takes one-third of the harvest, leaving two-thirds to the sharecropper, another Nahuat. Moreover, the corn is delivered by truck to his doorstep, and he and his sons only have to carry the sacks of corn a short distance to the granary in their dwelling. Nacho explained that Alfonso's and Adrian's families keep the money they earn, and their wives prepare meals in separate kitchens. Adrian's wife, Esperanza, shares her kitchen with Nacho's daughters, Cinorina and Gabriela, when they come from Mexico City to pay a visit. Gabriela is the child Nacho had with his second wife, Manuela.

Nacho, Adrian, and Esperanza in Victoria's kitchen

Gabriela

Josefina, Victoria Alfonso, and corn granary

Nacho explained that he encouraged his two married sons to stay in his household by providing them with corn for the granary his daughters-in-law use to feed their families. I asked Nacho why he provided his married sons with corn, and he said: "Because I'd feel badly if I didn't give to my children. I feel it is important to give them corn so they won't be hungry, so they won't suffer. That's why I give it to them. I don't weep about sharing. I don't want to be big. Yes. I don't want to be big. I give it to them, like I tell them, so there will be corn, so they'll eat. When there isn't any, we'll suffer."

CHAPTER 3

Talcuaco

Nacho's account of Victoria's death mentions and alludes to a tangled history of human relationships and animosities reaching far back into Huitzilan's past. To untangle this history, I shall start with Victoria herself, who was the lineal descendant of a non-Indian, or mestiza, woman, Juana Gutierrez, who settled in Huitzilan during the second half of the nineteenth century. Juana Gutierrez probably referred to herself as one of the people of reason, or "gente de razón," the phrase that the mestizos of the community used for themselves when I arrived there in 1968.

Juana Gutierrez had come to Huitzilan from the area around Cuetzalan del Progreso, which is in another part of the northern sierra of Puebla. She may have left the Cuetzalan area because of Nahuat opposition to mestizo settlement. A small number of mestizos had migrated into Cuetzalan "during the first half of the nineteenth century."[1] They ran into Nahuat who opposed their encroachment in what may have been a local version of the War of the Castes taking place in many indigenous areas in Mexico during this period.[2] According to the historian Guy Thomson, the Nahuat Pala Agustín Dieguillo "organized an armed movement aimed at expelling non-Indians from their midst."[3] That movement lasted from the early 1860s to the mid-1890s,[4] the period when Juana Gutierrez moved into Huitzilan. In her new community, she apparently found more accepting Indians, who spoke the same dialect of Nahuat, and a climate where she could raise the same crops as in the Cuetzalan area: corn and, even more important, sugarcane. Juana Gutierrez brought with her many gold coins, which she used to buy land including the fourteen-hectare plot of Talcuaco.

Although Victoria was the lineal descendant of Juana Gutierrez, she grew up speaking Nahuat in her home. Her father's mother and

Talcuaco and Tacalot in 2004

her mother's parents were Nahuat, and so both of her parents spoke Nahuat in their home and taught the language to her. Victoria's paternal grandfather was Juana Gutierrez's grandson (daughter's son), Ponciano Bonilla, who was a mestizo. Ponciano Bonilla had married a mestiza woman and also sired a number of children with Nahuat women. One of these children was Victoria's father, whom mestizos often identified with his maternal rather than paternal surname. During my earlier fieldwork, the mestizos, or gente de razón, in Huitzilan tended to call the children of many mestizo fathers and Nahuat mothers by their maternal surname. The use of the maternal surname for the offspring of mixed unions is one example of how non-Indians have attempted to maintain a line between themselves and the Nahuat.

There were many animosities that existed prior to the arrival of the UCI in Huitzilan, and many, but not all, involved the members of these mestizo and Nahuat families. To begin with, Juana Gutierrez did not write a will, and so her children and grandchildren had to decide for themselves how to divide the land she had bought in Huitzilan with the gold coins she reputedly brought from the Cuetzalan area. Several mestizo descendants of Juana Gutierrez had fought over Talcuaco and other plots in her estate that included Taltempan, located near the cemetery at the south end of town.

To complicate the picture, other mestizo families settled in Huitzilan, coming from the highlands to the south, particularly from the Spanish-speaking community of Tetela de Ocampo. These settlers arrived soon after 1900, and among them was Coyote, the man who allegedly issued the order to the town hall president to call in the army to chop down the Talcuaco cornfield. Coyote's older brother and Ponciano Bonilla became the local representatives of Gabriel Barrios, whose political dominion included the northern sierra of Puebla from 1917 to 1930.[5] Coyote, the youngest of three Tetela brothers, believed he had rights of ownership in Talcuaco because his daughter had lived with and given birth to the children of one of Juana Gutierrez's mestizo descendants. Coyote's claim of ownership met stiff resistance from another of Juana Gutierrez's mestizo descendants. He was a gun collector who allegedly gave guns and ammunition to the UCI to get back at Coyote.

MAIN PROTAGONISTS

Names of the deceased appear in italics, and those who died in the violence have an asterisk (*) before their names. Ethnicity appears in parentheses.

Angelina—Victoria's mother (Nahuat)
*Ciro—Wrath's younger brother and member of the UCI (Nahuat)
*Clemencia—Victoria's sister who confronted the killers of her brother "Nacho" and died in the massacre (Nahuat)
Coyote—youngest of the three Tetela brothers, took a major role in trying to drive the UCI out of Huitzilan (mestizo)
*Dog—fought with Wolf over a woman and invited the UCI to Huitzilan (Nahuat)
Epifania—Nacho and Victoria's oldest daughter (Nahuat)
*Eugenia—Victoria's other sister, who joined Clemencia in confronting their brother's killer and died in the massacre (Nahuat)
*Florentino—Victoria's oldest brother, member of the UCI and victim of the massacre (Nahuat)
Gallant—Coyote's nephew (BroSo) (mestizo)
*Juan—Victoria's father and UCI (Nahuat)
Juana Gutierrez—early settler who purchased Talcuaco and Taltempan in the nineteenth century (mestiza)
Nacho Angel—Victoria's husband and narrator of Remembering Victoria (Nahuat)
*"Nacho"—Victoria's brother and UCI, who died in a fight over a pistol (Nahuat)
Ponciano—Juana Gutierrez's grandson (DaSo) and Victoria's grandfather (FaFa) (mestizo)

Rake—Coyote's nephew (BroSo), who supported the UCI because of a quarrel with his uncle over family honor (mestizo)
Victoria—Nacho's wife, Ponciano's granddaughter (FaSo), who died in the massacre (Nahuat)
Wolf—fought with Dog over a woman and allied with Coyote (Nahuat)
Wrath—fought with Wolf after separating from Wolf's sister and joined Dog in inviting the UCI to Huitzilan to deal with Wolf (Nahuat)

Despite the appearance of unity among the members of prominent mestizo families, Coyote and his nephews had developed fierce animosities, primarily over women. Rake, the son of Coyote's oldest brother, had gotten three of Coyote's daughters pregnant. Coyote wanted to kill Rake, and Rake found his opportunity to get back at his uncle when the UCI arrived in 1977. Rake, as well, allegedly gave guns and ammunition to the UCI in the hope they would kill Coyote's sons.

The Nahuat had conflicts and animosities of their own. Some of the more notable ones involved the Nahuat Wolf, the man who used violence to get the women he wanted even if they were attached to other men. Soon after I arrived in 1968, several Nahuat told me that Wolf, who was married to one Nahuat woman, had wanted another and had killed her suitor and the suitor's mother to get her. He spent a short time in jail and then reappeared in Huitzilan after a wealthy mestizo in Huitzilan allegedly bribed an official to gain his release. At that time, several Nahuat told me that Wolf would probably not kill again.

They were wrong. Wolf still wanted the woman, who was now in a relationship with a married Nahuat man. That man was Dog, who was Nacho's relative, and he lived in the house just above the Talcuaco cattle pasture. Dog complained to Nacho that Wolf had tried to kill him more than once over the woman, who also lived in the neighborhood of Talcuaco. Meanwhile, other Nahuat men had problems with Wolf, and one was Wrath, who had married Wolf's sister and then separated from her. The hypothesis circulating among the Nahuat I knew was that the separation had created bad blood between Wolf and Wrath.

Into this complicated history of wrongs and disputes stepped the UCI in 1977. The UCI had organized a land invasion in the neighboring community of Pahuatla, a one-hour walk from Huitzilan. Wrath, Dog, and several other Nahuat men went to Pahuatla and appealed to the UCI to come to Huitzilan and help them deal with Wolf. The UCI leader was Felipe Reyes, a mestizo from Veracruz. The name "Felipe Reyes" may have come from the Robin Hood character in a popular radio novella broadcast over XEW into the northern sierra of Puebla. Felipe Reyes came to Huitzilan and held several meetings in homes and in secluded areas to organize the cooperative that invaded Talcuaco and Taltempan. Later on, the UCI became more public and organized marches through the streets of Huitzilan and at least one public rally in the cleared space in front of the church in the center of town.

Land Pressure

Many attended these meetings and the rallies because, in Nacho's opinion, they thought Felipe Reyes might help them do something about severe land shortages. The land situation for the Nahuat in Huitzilan was critical, as I discovered eight years prior to the appearance of Felipe. Reyes in the northern sierra of Puebla. In 1969, I hired a man who had ambiguous ethnicity and very good relations with the Nahuat to do a census of the community. He counted 2,273 women, children, and men who spoke Nahuat in the home, and 275 who spoke Spanish in the home. I am calling the first group "Nahuat" and the second group of non-Indians "mestizos" throughout this book. The 2,273 Nahuat lived in 438 domestic groups and owned just 97.3 hectares of privately held land.

In addition to private land, the municipality of Huitzilan at that time also had four parcels of ejido land, which prior to 1992 belonged to the federal government, which granted use rights to individuals, or "ejiditarios." One of the four ejido plots was in the valley of Huitzilan, and it had a total of 27.2 hectares. The ejiditarios of this plot had tiny parcels of one-fifth of a hectare, sufficient only for building a house and planting a few coffee trees. The Nahuat living in the valley of Huitzilan had access to two other small ejido parcels: one of 8.5 and the other of 5.5 hectares. The fourth plot was much larger, consisting of 295 hectares, most of which went to ejiditarios living in the settlements of Chachaloyan and Totutla at the southern end of the municipality.

The 438 Nahuat households had an average of 0.32 hectares of private and ejido land, which is far less than the minimum of one hectare of the best land required to grow one year's supply of corn for a small extended family of two married couples. The Nahuat prefer that their sons "work for one endeavor," or "ce cosa tequitih," after marriage by pooling the fruits of their labor in a common corn granary. Many households had at least two married couples, and several had more than two when I carried out the survey in 1969.

Felipe Reyes arrived in Huitzilan in 1977, when the situation was probably worse due to the increase in population and more mestizo land purchases. One symptom of the effect of land pressure on the Nahuat was tension in gender relations. I had detected this tension by comparing how Nahuat men in Huitzilan represented women in stories relative to Nahuat men in Yaonáhuac, a community in another part of the northern sierra with a more equitable distribution of land. Moreover, just before the UCI arrived in Huitzilan, many Nahuat living on the ejido of tiny plots averaging one-fifth of a hectare had converted from Catholicism to Protestantism. Their turning to another religion is one more indication that just prior to the appearance of the UCI the Nahuat were beginning to splinter from the effects of land pressure. Conversion to Protestantism meant breaking the ties of ritual kinship, or "compadrazgo," they had created with other Nahuat and some mestizos during their marriages and the baptisms of their children.

The Land Invasion

Under the leadership of Felipe Reyes, forty Nahuat men armed themselves and invaded the cattle pastures of Talcuaco and Taltempan. From any part of the Huitzilan valley, one could look up toward the mountains in the east and see the men of the UCI, dressed in their gleaming white cotton shirts and loose-fitting trousers, working their green cornfield on Talcuaco. Periodically, the state militia, dressed in black uniforms, would descend from the highlands by truck into the neighboring town of Pahuatla and walk the rest of the way into Huitzilan. The troops donned plastic shields and charged up the slope toward Talcuaco. The fleet-footed Nahuat working on Talcuaco scurried up over the mountains to safety on the other side. There, they could blend in with other Nahuat working their corn and bean fields on the fertile land of Xinachapan (Place of the Corn Seeds).

By this time, the Nahuat and the mestizos in Huitzilan had become bitterly divided along the lines of the animosities mentioned earlier. On one side were the mestizos Coyote and his immediate family (sons and grandchildren), and the Nahuat Wolf, who had fought with and killed other Nahuat men for the women he desired. On the other side were the UCIs, who included the Nahuat Dog, Wolf's rival for the woman who lived in the locality of Talcuaco near the disputed cattle pasture. Joining the UCI was also the Nahuat Wrath, who had married Wolf's

Photo of town from Talcuaco

sister and then separated from her. Allied with Dog and Wrath were mestizos who included Coyote's mestizo nephew, Rake, and at least one descendant of Juana Gutierrez who had fought with Coyote over Talcuaco. Other Nahuat joined these two factions out of kinship loyalty and mutual interest. Wolf's full brother and his paternal half brother, also a Nahuat, joined him in his fight against the UCI. Dog's sons and two of Wrath's brothers joined the UCI, as did some of Victoria's brothers and her father. Also in the UCI was one of the brothers of the Nahuat woman who was the object of the dispute between Wolf and Dog.

I ran into this woman's brother as he walked with the UCI in a procession down the main street of Huitzilan one evening in January of 1978. About forty Nahuat men, all from Huitzilan, walked silently and with solemn faces. Some carried .30-30 rifles, others held torches, and several painted slogans on the white walls of the mestizos' houses. The slogans read "Death to the Rich Ones" and "Land for Those Who Work It," the latter a phrase many attribute to the Mexican revolutionary hero Emiliano Zapata.[6] From Dog's house right above the Talcuaco pasture, one of Wrath's brothers broadcast through a loudspeaker speeches threatening death to the rich and repeating the slogan attributed to Zapata. He also played the same song over and over extolling the fallen insurgent leader Lucio Cabañas, who died in a clash with the army in 1974 in Guerrero.[7]

At first, the violence in Huitzilan was limited to clashes between the UCI and Wolf and his brothers. Eventually Wolf allegedly shot and killed Felipe Reyes, and the Nahuat in the UCI, who included Dog and Wrath, tried to kill Wolf and his brothers. I could feel the tension rising in Huitzilan and tried to stay out of the fray by visiting storytellers I had known from before. I left the village at the end of my fieldwork in 1978. The UCI planted several corn crops on Talcuaco and Taltempan and pursued Wolf until they killed him and his half brother.

Nacho described what happened next: "One day they broke up the milpa the UCI had planted. They cut down the entire milpa. From there, yes, that's when the rage, or cualayot, began. The UCI started killing. They became blind with rage. They started spying. They spied. Until they just killed even if their victims did not have fault. They killed secretly [they shot their victims in the back]."[8]

Coyote's niece identified who chopped down the Talcuaco cornfield. "I was in Huitzilan. I have in my memory the army coming into town. And the way Coyote's family became involved in the act of destroying the milpa. Using power to do so. There had not been any deaths, any wounded. At that moment the UCI did have arms and they displayed them at times. They used them in that way. Those people walked through the streets of the town with their weapons. They did not confront the army. Nevertheless they put up what we might call passive resistance. And the army had to use force to get them out of Talcuaco. Not by wounding anyone but. . . . And the family of Coyote acted with arrogance by gloating about what happened. They thought they were triumphant after what took place. They gathered the youngest members of the family, the grandchildren of Coyote and some other boys who worked for them who were from Wolf's family. Three or four young men from that family. They took active parts, they were physically there on the land when there was the eviction and the act of chopping down the milpa, destroying what was planted on the milpa. This was the spark. The indignation that caused in town! And it was the spark that caused the UCI to respond with violence."[9]

The UCI directed its anger toward the members of the town hall government, who included the president, a Nahuat, who allegedly was in league with Coyote, who took such a conspicuous role in trying to drive the UCI out of Huitzilan. Between 1979 and 1984, the UCI killed or tried to kill every official of the town hall, as well as many others who they suspected were enemies. Estimates of the number of dead vary. An editorial appearing in the newspaper *La Jornada* put the figure at one hundred.[10] A mestizo who was born and raised in Huitzilan and who knows the community well kept a list of all those who died during the violence, and he had written nearly three hundred names on his list before he had to leave the community because of extortion threats. The Web site of the Antorcha Campesina, the group affiliated with the PRI that has governed Huitzilan since February 1984, described the violence as producing "rivers of blood."[11] Many also fled from the community because they feared the UCI. In 1982 and 1983, the schools closed after a Nahuat in the UCI killed the brother of the school principal, who then picked up the keys to the school and left the village with his family. Nahuat in the UCI died or fled when the Antorcha, together with Nahuat who had been living in exile, retook the village in late 1983 and early 1984.

The National and Global Context

Land invasions involving other Nahuas living on the edge of the Central Mexican Plateau near the Gulf Coast had taken place earlier in the 1970s. Frans Schryer reported on land invasions occurring in the Huasteca of Hidalgo as early as 1971. Schryer noted that the Huasteca invasions began during the regime of the Mexican president Luis Echeverría (1970–1976), who "reactivated agrarianism on a national level, using much the same rhetoric as Cárdenas in the thirties." Under Echeverría, the state mobilized peasants against ranchers, setting the stage for "new groups of militant peasants in a region that was ripe for rebellion."[12] One of those groups was the UCI, which originated in Veracruz and appeared in the northern sierra right after Echeverría left office in 1976.

Among the reasons for land invasions in the Huasteca were cultural values and the unequal distribution of land. Schryer is careful to point out that class and ethnicity did not necessarily coincide in Huejutla, where "poor peasants from many Nahua communities not only took part in land invasions directed against outsiders, but they were also involved in open (and often violent) conflicts" with other Nahuas.[13] He reported that in 1971, "a group of poor peasants who had access only to a badly eroded hillside invaded a pasture belonging to the richest Nahua family in Pepeyocatitla."[14] Schryer added that cultural values justified participation in the Pepeyocatitla rebellion, noting that poor Nahuas "reinterpreted or utilized traditional Indian values to defend their class interests and to transform internal class relations." Among the ways those values found expression were "communal land boundaries."[15]

The land invasions that took place in the Nahua areas of the Huasteca de Hidalgo and the northern sierra of Puebla occurred at about the same time as unrest was developing in other parts of Mexico and Central America. In the 1970s, the Guerrilla Army of the Poor, or EGP, began operating in the Mayan-speaking areas of Guatemala. Like Felipe Reyes, their leaders were also mestizos, and they recruited Mayans, many of whom lived in regions as remote as the northern sierra of Puebla. These regions tended to be mountainous areas where Mesoamericans could escape from Spanish and mestizo settlers until the nineteenth century. At that time, mestizos began moving into indigenous areas, as they did in the northern sierra of Puebla, and soon acquired the bulk of the land and became the dominant group economically, socially, and politically.

The structural conditions contributing to the violence that erupted in these areas during the 1970s and 1980s included the shortage of land for people who valued working together to fill a granary to feed the members of their extended families. Scholars have argued about why the speakers of indigenous languages become involved in Maoist groups of this period. The arguments focus on what some have called the solidarity position, according to which insurgency develops among Mesoamericans as a reaction to their oppression. David Stoll argued against the solidarity position, contending that the Ixil joined the EGP not to fight oppression but because of previous animosities and in reaction to attacks by the Guatemalan army provoked by the EGP itself.[16] Beatríz Manz, however, found evidence among the K'iche' she interviewed supporting the solidarity position. Her informants reported that they did indeed join the EGP to fight against their oppressors.[17]

Important Symbols

It appears from the Guatemalan and Mexican cases that the structural conditions that can lead to these small, but nevertheless very bloody, wars exist in many places, but do not necessarily erupt in violence. Moreover, the reasons, the timing, and the form of the violence appear to vary from one case to the next. Much depends on the particular histories of each community, and for those histories it is necessary to turn to the people who lived through them. Their testimonies, coupled with my earlier fieldwork, led me to conclude that Huitzilan was a tense field of forces before the UCI arrived in Huitzilan. The troubles between Wolf and Dog, and Coyote and Juana Gutierrez's descendants, to mention just a few of the cases, were some of the lines of cleavage by which Huitzilan came apart following the Talcuaco and Taltempan land invasions.

The spark, however, that detonated the rage, or cualayot, was the very important symbolic act of chopping down the UCI's cornfield in full view of the entire community. To understand the meaning of that act, it will help to consider how Nahuat and mestizos regard land and corn. For the Nahuat, land is something one works to produce food, and for mestizos it is a commodity. The Nahuat personify the earth as a woman and the young corn plant as a young man. The mestizos value corn as a food for themselves and their animals, but they do not personify the corn plant in the way the Nahuat do.

To understand more fully the Nahuat point of view, it may help to turn to the narratives that circulated in Huitzilan oral tradition before the UCI had arrived. These stories were told out of earshot of mestizos, even those who could speak Nahuat fluently. One very popular story was "Blancaflor," and Nacho's version contains a very revealing image of the meaning of land to a Nahuat narrator. The character of Blancaflor is historically derived from Medea, who enabled Jason to perform the incredible tasks demanded by her father as a condition for obtaining the golden fleece.[18] Nacho told a version of this story in 1970 and described how the heroine, Blancaflor, helps her lover, Juan, perform incredible tasks her father had demanded of him. One of the tasks is to clear a field stretching to the horizon, plant it with chiles, and harvest a sack of them in a single day.[19] She smacks the earth with her hand, making a noise like a baby smacking its lips while nursing at the mother's breast, calling forth ants from under the ground, and they do the work with incredible speed. When Nacho told this story, he said Blancaflor "started to make a smacking noise on the earth with her hand." He used the phrase "pehuac talcocomotza imai." The word talcocomotza is a compound of the noun tal (earth or land) and cocomotza, a verb describing a baby's "smacking noise nursing at the breast."[20]

The image of the earth or land (tal) as a woman's breast is related to many other images of the earth as a woman's body in Nahuat mythology of the pre-UCI period. For example, Miguel Ahuata told a creation myth of two brothers, one who stayed home to prepare meals and the other who planted a milpa in the forest. The act of planting produced both the Nahuat, who populated Huitzilan, and their food, the corn that filled their granary.[21] In actual planting, a man makes holes in the moist earth with a long, pointed stick and inserts kernels of corn as if he were seating an infant in a woman's womb. The phrase "The infant is seated in the womb" is López Austin's translation of the sixteenth-century phrase for conception "I(h)tic motlalia in piltzintli."[22] The equation between planting and procreation is just one of many ways that the Nahuat of Huitzilan identify with the corn plant. Alan Sandstrom skillfully demonstrated how the Nahuatl of the Huasteca of Veracruz say that corn is food that provides the strength, or "chicahualiz," in their blood.[23] The Nahuat identification with the corn plant is part of their monism, or their belief that the universe is an organic whole. The monistic metaphysical foundation of the meaning the Nahuat attribute to land and corn was at the center of the Talcuaco dispute.

Consequently, chopping down the corn plants infuriated the Nahuat in and outside of the UCI for several reasons. Destroying corn plants before they had a chance to yield a crop was like attacking the Nahuat themselves. It destroyed an important food that produces the strength in a person's blood. It was an act of callous disrespect for the Nahuat who had worked on Talcuaco with the hope of harvesting corn to put into their granaries. It was a humiliating demonstration of power by a mestizo who had a reputation for coveting land and using tricks to obtain it.

The rage, or cualayot, that erupted over the Talcuaco cornfield is part of a much broader pattern of agrarian violence that breaks out when those who hold what June Nash calls collective worldviews clash with others who embrace the free market philosophies of Adam Smith and David Ricardo.[24] The form that clash can take, its timing, the degree of bloodshed, the lines of cleavage, and the splintering of Mesoamerican communities occur in different ways that do not easily reduce to a general principle.

Chapter 4 will present the testimonies of some mestizos and Nahuat who witnessed and experienced the clash in their community that erupted over Talcuaco. Their accounts will reveal and help explain the irony that Coyote's alleged act of calling in the army to chop down the cornfield, and sending his grandchildren to join the army, in full view of the entire community resulted in Nahuat fratricide rather than interethnic warfare. Coyote, who had lived most of his life in Huitzilan, humiliated the Nahuat, knowing how they regarded corn. The Nahuat reacted by splintering, as those in the UCI went after other Nahuat and eventually turned on each other in the massacre in which Victoria lost her life.

CHAPTER 4

Fratricide

The rage, or cualayot, meant different things to people in Huitzilan depending on their position in the social structure and their particular histories with the Nahuat who had become members of the UCI. For Nacho and other Nahuat in his community, the rage, which erupted when the army chopped down the Talcuaco cornfield, turned into fratricide more than interethnic warfare. Some, like Nacho, found themselves in the crosshairs of the UCI, at least one of whom carried a powerful R-15 assault rifle, the civilian version of the M-16, developed for the war in Vietnam and manufactured by Colt arms company. Others managed to stay clear of the fray, although few escaped untouched by tragedy during the years leading up to and including the demise of the UCI in the early months of 1984. The conflict that erupted after the army chopped down the Talcuaco milpa was complicated and involved mestizos as well as Nahuat, resulting in a near-total breakdown of the social order.

Despite the sharp ethnic boundaries in Huitzilan, oral histories collected between 2003 and 2005 do not support the idea that a war between Nahuat and mestizos broke out in Huitzilan. To be sure, the UCI shot, wounded, and killed a few mestizos for having harassed Nahuat women, and for having humiliated Nahuat men, as well as for taking a leading role in driving the UCI off Talcuaco. However, the conflict became very violent because some mestizos worked with the UCI to carry out vendettas against other mestizos over Talcuaco and Taltempan. A lineal descendant of Juana Gutierrez was a gun collector, and he gave the R-15 and other weapons and ammunition to the UCI to get back at Coyote for trying to grab Talcuaco. Coyote's nephew alluded to this conflict when he attributed it to a problem of land ownership. Rake also allegedly gave guns and ammunition and perhaps money to the UCI to get back at his uncle, Coyote, who wanted to kill him for getting three of his daughters pregnant.

The UCI was an entirely Nahuat group following the death of its Veracruz leader, Felipe Reyes. Nahuat leaders of the UCI maintained respectful relationships with certain members of Coyote's family, particularly during the early phase of the conflict over Talcuaco. One such local UCI leader was Wrath, the Nahuat who asked Felipe Reyes to come to Huitzilan and who twice came to the church, allegedly to kill Nacho. Wrath had worked for many years with Coyote's nephew, whom Nacho and I shall call Gallant, and his wife, whom I shall call Hope, who ran one of the larger stores in Huitzilan. Wrath's brothers, who took active roles in the UCI, also had good relations with this mestizo family. Gallant and Hope's oldest son, Alonso, recalled how he was able to dissuade Wrath's younger brother, Ciro, from killing Wolf's brother, whom the UCI had cornered in Gallant and Hope's store. Wolf was one of the reasons Dog, Wrath, and other Nahuat had gone to Pahuatla and asked Felipe Reyes, the UCI leader from Veracruz, to come to Huitzilan.

Ciro and other Nahuat in the UCI were on the porch of and inside Gallant and Hope's store, standing along the long wooden counter drinking beer, when they spotted Wolf leave Coyote's store, two houses to the north, and walk down the main street toward them. Wolf might have seen them and turned back immediately if he had not been drunk. When the UCI members spotted Wolf, they dashed out of the store, ran across the street, circled around through the coffee orchard, and appeared on the coffee-drying platform directly in front of and across the main street from Gallant's father's house. Gallant's father was the middle of the three Tetela brothers, who included Coyote and Rake's father. The UCIs pointed their rifles at Wolf as he passed directly in front of them on the other side of the street. Wolf had his back against the wall of the house that belonged to Gallant's father and stood between Coyote's house to the north and Gallant's store to the south. For a moment, Wolf did not know whether he should draw his gun or try to escape. He crept along the wall, facing his enemies, who hesitated to fire their weapons as they argued among themselves about whom they had assigned to kill their enemy. Wolf found his opportunity to escape when he realized he had reached the open front door of Gallant's father's house. He darted inside and apparently escaped through the back door, and the UCIs, realizing they had lost their opportunity to kill him, headed toward the center of town to the south. Meanwhile, Wolf's brother appeared in the narrow alley that separated Gallant's store from his father's house, and caught the eye of Ciro just as he was leaving with the rest of his companions. Gallant had left Huitzilan for supplies, leaving Hope and her oldest son, Alonso, to tend the store. Alonso described what happened, and his description reveals the degree to which important Nahuat members of the UCI respected his family despite their close kinship with Coyote:

A group of at least eight or ten people came to the house. They were all armed. Or most were, and they carried what are known commonly as long arms; there were some muskets, a rifle, perhaps a small machine gun, and they also carried pistols. They all came armed. They came to the house. On that day, it seems to me that my father wasn't here. They came to the house. They ordered some beers. They usually arrived and ordered and drank beers and usually did not pay for them. They didn't say it was an obligation to give them beer. Rather, they said for me to put it on their bill. That is to say, they never paid for them. This is to give you a little idea of what their conduct was like. Not to defend the value of the beer. Then, we, my mother and I, were helping in the store. We didn't know what they were up to at that moment. They probably knew that Wolf was going to pass by there. Yes, it seems to me they knew he was in my Uncle Coyote's house at that moment. Well, you know their locations. You know that my uncle's house is very close. The UCI were inside the store or on the porch of my house. They drank some beer, and, at that moment, Wolf came down the street. As if a child or some children had given him the message that some person was waiting for him in my father's store. As you well know, the store is situated in such a way that there is a small alley which separates our store from my grandfather's house. And people were hiding in this alley, and some others went around the house through the orchard of Grandfather's house, and through to the coffee-drying porch on the opposite side of the street. When Wolf appeared, when he was walking down the street, the people came out and pointed their guns at him. I don't know if he was armed. But obviously he did not have a chance to pull out his gun. And he didn't try to. Wolf went back quickly, he walked backwards while his ambushers, his enemies, were aiming at him. They all had long arms, and some had pistols.

Meanwhile, I went out to the porch of the store, and they were saying in Nahuat, it seems they said to Dog, "Kill him. You're the one who has to kill him."

Dog: "No. Kill him yourself. You're the one responsible and you have to kill him."

Then Wolf pressed against the wall, with the guns very close to him, certainly just a few meters away, and he went back until he found the entrance to

Grandfather's house. As you know, the doors of the houses in towns, at least in the past, and especially in Huitzilan, they always remain open. The doors aren't kept closed as in the cities. Then he saved himself because, when they were pointing at him from very close, he decided to jump inside and push the door closed. They couldn't shoot him there. In the first place, his enemies wouldn't go shooting in a house that didn't belong to the person who was their target. And in the second place, I don't know if he went into some of the rooms, crawled under the beds, or possibly continued running through the back to the orchard, where there is a path toward what they call Calpolaco [Place of the Submerged House]. I think he took the path toward that place. He was drunk. Well, obviously they spread out looking for him. Some went around Grandfather's house, but obviously the people who were in Grandfather's house, they didn't just let them go search inside the house. Presumably someone told Wolf's brother that Wolf was somewhere about. Surely there was a rumor they had killed him, or something like that. Then Wolf's brother appeared in the alley that goes to the stable of my father's house. The UCI had already gone, nearly all of them had gone toward the center of town, and then Ciro happened to see him. Ciro was very young. He was one of Wrath's brothers. Ciro was almost my contemporary. He is two years older, but we played marbles together, and in school, we played with slingshots and with everything that one plays with in Huitzilan. So then Ciro stayed back, and he turned to say good-bye to me, because we always spoke to each other, and then he saw Wolf's brother appear. I saw that Ciro came back, and he pointed a pistol. And he said to Wolf's brother, if I remember correctly, he said in Hispanicized Nahuat: "We're looking for your brother, you son of the fucked mother." ["Tictemotih mocniuh hijo de la chingada."] And he pointed the pistol at him.

And then I said to him, "Look Ciro, no, no, no. You're in my house."

Ciro: "But this son of the fucked mother, and also his brother, he's also participated in the killings, in the slaughters, in the ambushes."

At this moment, Wolf's brother took advantage of a brief moment in Ciro's distraction and put himself directly inside the store. I don't remember if he went in over near where the corn is [the house's entrance] or if he jumped over the counter, but he went into the store next to my mother.

Then my mother stood next to him, and she said, "Don't kill him."

And then I tried to calm Ciro, telling him, "Look, Ciro, we know each other. I'm neither your enemy nor am I on his side. But you're in my house, and look at my mother, who is next to him. How are you going to shoot?" I said something like that to him.

Ciro: "All right. It's true. We know each other and we're friends."

And I don't remember exactly what he said to Wolf's brother. He said, more or less, in Nahuat, "We'll find you again, son of the fucked mother."

This mestizo's testimony reveals that during the UCI's time in Huitzilan, relations across ethnic lines were very variable and particularistic.[1] The variable and particularistic relations are one reason that the cultural differences between the Nahuat and the mestizos did not turn the rage (cualayot) into interethnic warfare. Interethnic relations in Huitzilan differed from one case to the next during the earlier period of fieldwork (1968–1978), and some of the patterns that had developed prior to the appearance of the UCI continued afterwards, as Alonso revealed in his account of Ciro. One of the reasons that Alonso was able to restrain Ciro from shooting Wolf's brother was because Alonso and Ciro had a good relationship, and Ciro respected both Alonso and his mother, Hope, from before 1977. I think Ciro respected Alonso and his mother because of the way Alonso's mother taught her children to play down class differences and take into consideration the feelings of the Nahuat. She told me at about the time I recorded Alonso's testimony: "Above all they had to be the equal of the indigenous people here, be their equals. As if there were no class differences. I always told them that. I think that was something very important. If I were to see them eating candy, I said, 'Share it. And if you're not going to share any, then don't eat it in front of someone.'"

The act of eating in front of another without sharing may seem like a trivial matter, but it has great importance to the Nahuat. As mentioned earlier, the Nahuat pool the fruits of milpa labor to fill a corn granary from which all women in the household can draw to feed their families. Sharing food is part of the moral economy of the household that is based on the concept of respect, or "icnoyot." Thus, to eat in front of another is to act without taking into consideration the feelings of another and is consequently an act of disrespect. Because Gallant and Hope brought up their children to have respeto for others, the Nahuat responded in kind. The shared culture implied in the meanings icnoyot and respeto have in common is one reason that Gallant and Hope have ties of compadrazgo with several Nahuat families in the village.

Moreover, Gallant kept a low political profile, he did not fool around with or harass Nahuat women, he did not own any land, and so he did not have enemies in the community. He tried to maintain his independence by transporting the victims in both warring groups to the hospital in Zacapoaxtla. His children followed suit, as Alonso revealed in his oral history when he told how he presented himself to Ciro as unpartisan in the conflict over Wolf's brother. According to Alonso, he was able to convince Ciro that he was truly neutral, a stance that some members of the UCI respected in mestizos.

The Fratricide

The Nahuat in the UCI turned their sights on other Nahuat for many reasons that included fights over women and siding or appearing to side with Coyote. Deep divisions developed among the Nahuat in Huitzilan, as Nacho explained when he said: "At first, the UCI didn't do anything. But afterwards, well, they started fighting our brothers." ["Primero ahmo tei quichihuayah. Pero zatepa pos pehuac quintehuiayah tocnihuan."] The phrase "our brothers," or "tocnihuan," refers to all Nahuat living in Huitzilan, who should have respect, or icnoyot, and not fight with each other. Quintehuiayah can mean "they fought against them" or "they hated them," according to the Nahuat dictionary that Harold Key and Mary Ritchie de Key compiled in nearby Xalacapan, close to Zacapoaxtla.[2] For hate, Nacho used the nouns for rage or anger: cualayot and tahhueliliz. Unlike the vocabulary of Spanish and English, there is no Nahuat noun for hate that is the opposite of love, or tazohtaliz. The Nahuat indicate hate by the action of physically fighting with or being angry with another. In this sense, the rage, or cualayot, represented a severe challenge to Nacho's idealized code of conduct, according to which one should maintain respect, love, and compassion.

Nacho explained that he could not easily tell from the demeanor of the Nahuat in the UCI that they considered him one of their enemies. He described how he had cordial relations with Dog, whose house above Talcuaco was the group's headquarters during the early phases of the land invasion. It was from Dog's house that the UCI broadcast its slogans "death to the rich" and "land is for those who work it." Nacho knew Dog well and believed that they had a special connection because their ancestors were born on the same plot of land, Taltzintan, which means "Land at the Foot" of Talcuaco. Nacho explained his relationship to Dog in the following way: "He was our relative. From where I came, he was from where my grandmother came, from where my father came. We were from one stalk." Nacho used the word tactzon (stalk), which is a combination of tacti, or torso, and tzonti, or head of hair.[3] Nacho defined tactzon as the stalk of a plant because he, like the ancient[4] as well as contemporary Nahuas,[5] identifies the human body with the corn plant. Regarding the ancient Nahuas, López Austin noted that the word tonacayo (the whole of our flesh) "is applied to the fruits of the earth, especially to the most important one, corn, thus forming a metaphoric tie between man's corporeal being and the food to which he owed his existence."[6]

Nacho told how Dog spoke to him frankly and warmly, explaining why he felt compelled to join the UCI because of a fight with Wolf over a woman.

> One time I went to Dog's house, he was already with the UCI, and I was looking for some medicine. So then my wife said he sold vitamins.
>
> Victoria: "Go see him."
>
> Nacho: "OK, I'll go to see him."
>
> I arrived at his house. It was as if I didn't have a problem with him. They received me. They invited me to drink coffee. Dog and I talked. And that's when he started telling me, he said:
>
> "I wouldn't have joined them. I wouldn't have joined them. But this man [Wolf], every time I see him, it's important that he shoot me. Wherever we meet, it's important for him to shoot me. So then, that's why I went in with them, so he wouldn't shoot me."
>
> That's why. And it was for that woman. Sometimes Wolf was stupid. He had his wife. He also wanted the other woman to be his wife. Why did he want another one so he and Dog would fight over her? He was disrespectful, he did a disrespectful thing.

However, Nacho soon discovered that there is a big difference between semblance and reality when he had his first encounter with Wrath in the beautiful domed church in the center of Huitzilan. Nacho's account of that encounter reveals several things about the rhetoric among the Nahuat as they became more deeply divided as the UCI was gaining the upper hand in Huitzilan during the last months of Nacho's term as justice of the peace (1979–1981). Wrath accused Nacho of "acting big," or hueichihua, a phrase that means to act egotistically rather than in accord with the demands of the group. To act big goes against respect, or icnoyot, which parents try to inculcate in their children, so they will work for the family. To refuse to "work for one endeavor," or ce cosa tequitih, often means to act out of self-interest, one form of acting big. Such accusations frequently occur among family members who are in the process of dividing the granary and working separately. In using this phrase, Wrath alluded to Nacho's refusing to join the UCI and to his continuing service as justice of the peace in the town hall, whose president had allegedly sided with Coyote. By the end of Nacho's term as justice of the peace, the band now known as the UCI harbored resentment against those who did not join them in the original group of forty.

Nacho tried to dissuade Wrath from killing him by reminding him that they had worked together on the same milpa. As Catherine Good observed, the Nahua generally equate work with love and say that those who work together love each other.[7] Nacho was attempting to trigger Wrath's memory of having worked together in the past so that he might recall this experience of love, or tazohtaliz, that they shared before the arrival of the UCI in Huitzilan. However, Wrath was unconvinced, because, as Nacho explained, relations had deteriorated between the Nahuat in the UCI and those who had not joined the cooperative, and particularly those who served in the town hall government after the army chopped down the Talcuaco milpa. It is possible, even likely, that Wrath concluded that Nacho and other Nahuat did not love them because they refused to work in their cooperative during the UCI agrarian phase in Huitzilan. Also, as Nacho pointed out, Wrath told of unknown men shooting at him, and he suspected anyone affiliated with the town hall government at that time. Nacho's narrative also reveals that Wrath was concerned about locating the guns rumored to exist in the town hall. The supply of arms and ammunition had become a critical concern to members of the UCI, who had few resources and depended on mestizos carrying vendettas against other mestizos for their firepower. Quarrels over guns among the members of the UCI band would become a serious issue later on when the Antorcha Campesina, the group affiliated with the PRI, started its campaign to drive the UCI out of Huitzilan.

Nacho's narrative also reveals how Victoria acted with courage to confront Wrath face-to-face in part because she could invoke the name of her father, who was one of the senior-most members of the group. Wrath and other Nahuat knew the story of Victoria's father fighting with and killing the suitor of his daughter, Clemencia, for failing to act with respect. He also knew, as did many Nahuat as well as mestizos, that Victoria's father was a man who acted on strong passions and, like many Nahuat fathers, was very protective of his daughters. Wrath may have known that Victoria's father was fond of and willing to protect Nacho.

The situation got worse for Nacho and Victoria as the UCI killed off more members of the town hall government. After shooting the Nahuat who allegedly was in league with Coyote, the UCI also killed another Nahuat who took his place as president, despite the fact that he apparently had nothing to do with calling in the army to chop down the Talcuaco milpa several years earlier. By then, Nacho was ending his three-year term as justice of the peace and was facing more threats from Wrath; he eventually concluded it was no longer possible for him to walk safely in Huitzilan. He decided to work in Mexico City, feeling that as long as Victoria's father was still alive, the UCI was unlikely to harm Victoria in his absence.

Estimates vary as to the size of the UCI at the time the group roamed without much opposition in Huitzilan, but one mestizo, who had good relations with the Nahuat and drank with UCIs, made an estimate based on the number of beers he had to order for them. This mestizo began by noting that UCI members had organized themselves into three armed groups, one for each of the three regions of the community. He recalled the time he and a friend ran into the group from the north when it ventured into the center of town. The UCIs in the northern group proposed drinking beer at one of the stores near the church. The mestizo agreed, but what he did not know was that the northern group had sent word to the other groups to join the drinking party. He explained that he had ordered two cases of beer, with twenty bottles in each case, for a total of forty beers. He described what happened next. "And when I ordered, already there were several more than before. And there wasn't enough beer in all of the cases. There were forty-two, forty-three, that is more than forty. And I had to ask for more."

Arrival of the Antorcha

The violence reached a new level when the Antorcha Campesina appeared in the village in 1983. This is how one mestizo from Huitzilan described its arrival.

One day they arrived in some pickup trucks. They asked the people of Huitzilan for arms. They asked some people for money to buy arms, to lend them arms. They armed themselves. The leaders were people who had nothing to do with Huitzilan. They belong to the Secretariat of Agriculture and Water Resources. In those days, they were SARH and people who worked in the CONASUPO basically.

SARH is an acronym for the Secretary of Agriculture and Hydraulic Resources. The CONASUPO is a system of government-run stores all over the country that provide staples at low cost. This witness continued:

In Zacapoaxtla, there were a lot of people who had fled from Huitzilan. Zacapoaxtla was the natural place of refuge for Huitzilan, a place where the Huitziltecos could find a way to survive, sweeping the streets, carrying burdens, or working as laborers. Then from among the leaders who were not from there, they brought a political plan, and it met the needs of all of those refugees. Almost all of them had been threatened. The UCI had killed a close relative, and they had felt obliged to leave the village. It was easy to convince them, "We're going to give you arms and we're going in to take the town and chase the UCI out."

So they arrived on the twenty-first of March and began to have their first armed clashes where they killed some of the UCI. One of the first clashes was when the Antorcha had just arrived, and I think the former head of the UCI died, and it seems to me another couple of people in the strongest face-to-face clash. It seems to me it took place on lands near where Rake lived, thereabouts.

One can reconstruct some aspects of the regional and Puebla state context around the time that the Antorcha appeared in Huitzilan in October of 1983, with the aid of newspaper articles as well as oral interviews. A look at the chronology of events reveals that the Antorcha appeared in Huitzilan in late September or in early October of 1983, just before the town hall elections, scheduled to take place on November 27 in Huitzilan and elsewhere throughout the state of Puebla. By that time, the UCI had lost its hold in the communities immediately surrounding Huitzilan. Opponents had jailed some of the UCI leaders from the neighboring town of Pahuatla on June 16, 1981,[8] and allegedly thrown others to the sharks swimming off the nearby Gulf Coast. In the fall of 1982, the governor of Puebla, Guillermo Jimenez Morales, of the PRI, visited the communities adjacent to Huitzilan, congratulating them on their civic-mindedness and offering them money for public works.[9] It is significant that he did not mention Huitzilan or the problems in that community in any of the speeches reported in the press. Apparently he was making routine visits and promises in preparation for the town hall elections scheduled for November 27, 1983. The PRI expected to win most of those elections, but newspaper reports indicated that it faced opposition from the PSUM, the United Socialist Party of Mexico, in the thirty-five

Chronology

	Nacho	Huitzilan	Puebla	Mexico
1968		Fieldwork begins		Tlatelolco massacre
1970	Nacho marries Victoria			Echeverría is president
1971	First Adrian is born			Pepeyocatitla land invasion in Huasteca of Hidalgo
1973	Epifania is born			
1975	Alfonso is born			
1977		UCI invades Talcuaco and Taltempan in Huitzilan	UCI invades land in Pahuatla	UCI demands land reform
1978	Cinorina is born			UCI demands release of 13 political prisoners Press reports 250 invasions in 1977–1978
1979	Nacho becomes justice of peace	Rake becomes town hall president		
1980	Second Adrian is born			
1981			3 UCI leaders from Pahuatla jailed	
1982		UCI governs Huitzilan	Protest march in Zacapoaxtla demanding release of 3 UCI leaders Governor visits Zongozotla and Zapotitlán Governor promises public works for Xochitlán hamlets	López Portillo is president

Continued

	Nacho	Huitzilan	Puebla	Mexico
1983	Juanito is born			
	Father-in-law is killed			
	Nacho goes to Zacapoaxtla		Municipio	
	Victoria dies on October 15		elections on November 27	
	Nacho takes children to Zacapoaxtla			
1984	Nacho and children return in March	Antorcha takes the Huitzilan town hall in February		

municipios in the northern sierra of Puebla, where the UCI along with other groups had "confronted oppression" for five years.[10] It seems reasonable to conclude that the Antorcha, which is affiliated with the PRI, chose a propitious time to go into Huitzilan and drive out the UCI.

Death of Victoria's Father

One of those who probably fell to an Antorcha bullet in one of the first battles was Nacho's father-in-law. Nacho did not witness his death and did not know for sure the identity of the murderer, but he believed that enemies "killed my father-in-law because he was a UCI" ["quimictiqueh nomontaht, bueno porque UCI catca"]. According to one mestizo, who was near the scene, Nacho's father-in-law died when he ran to the aid of his UCI companions when he heard shots of the battle. The mestizo reported: "We were collecting on the advances that the Coffee Institute had given out. Then that's when one heard the shots. Nacho's father-in-law was also collecting. And he ran off. He wanted to help his companions but he was shot." This account of Nacho's father-in-law as an enthusiastic supporter of the UCI, who was willing to pick up his rifle and defend his companions at the cost of his life, does not accord with the way Nacho remembers his explaining why he joined up with the

UCI. His father-in-law had told him that he joined the insurgent group so he would not be punished for killing his daughter's suitor several years earlier.

Nacho Goes to Zacapoaxtla

With the death of his father-in-law, Nacho felt he had to leave Huitzilan and join many from his village who sought refuge from the UCI by living in Zacapoaxtla. Shortly after leaving his village, he learned of the massacre in which Victoria perished, along with her sisters, Clemencia and Eugenia, and their brother, Florentino. Because Nacho was not in Huitzilan when the massacre took place, I turned to the mestizo who earlier had helped me do a census of the village in 1969. He liked to drink with the UCI. He gave his account of the circumstances that led to Victoria's death on the afternoon of October 15, 1983. He also accompanied the group that inspected the macabre murder scene on the morning of the following day.

The Massacre

This witness described how he was a member of the work team, or "faena," assigned the task of cleaning up the cemetery in time for the Day of the Dead celebration that would begin on the last day of October. His account begins on the day Victoria died.

We went to do public work on the cemetery and on the way back we stopped and were drinking in the house of Fulano at the south end of town. In the little store out on the street. So then other UCI came, they had come to tell the UCIs drinking at the little store that the Antorchas had arrived. And so then they stopped drinking and got their guns ready. They spread out. They came here by the gully. They went down by the Pereañezes' [this mestizo, like many others, tended to use Victoria's father's maternal surname]. And we came here to the center of town. And we started to hear gunshots. We could only hear the shots because they were from down there at Nacho's father-in-law's house. And in the afternoon, when it was very late, it was known that they had killed those three sisters and a brother. And there was nothing we could do. We couldn't go. We were afraid they would be there spying, watching to see who went to see the victims.

Inspecting the Murder Scene

Then the next day we went. I and my compadre and some others went along with Manuel Mina [a Nahuat who was town hall president] to see the dead bodies. We went to collect them. And yes, we went fearing they would be watching to see who would come. We only went to collect the dead bodies. They ordered coffins to bury them the next day. Clemencia was inside at the foot of her sewing machine. And her sister Victoria and her brother, Florentino, were on the coffee-drying floor outside. And Victoria was with her child.

This witness forgot to mention Eugenia, who also died in the massacre. After the tape recorder was turned off, he added that Juanito was attempting to nurse from Victoria's breast.

Epifania Remembers

Nacho and Victoria's oldest child, Epifania, was nine years old when her mother died. In 2006, she remembered that her mother had left her and her brother in their Talcez home while she went to visit her mother in Miyacaco,[11] at the southern end of town.

It wasn't long after my mother had arrived at Grandmother's house in Miyacaco. We heard them start shooting and we wondered what was going on. I was very frightened, as were the neighbors. They asked, "Where did your mother go?"

"She went to Grandmother's."

"There is a lot of shooting down there."

"Yes. And now what shall I do? My mother said, 'Now you wait here.'"

"Why did she go?"

"I don't know why she went. She wanted to go visit Grandmother, and she left us here."

And I really felt terrible because when they fired guns it was because they were shooting someone. They didn't shoot for just any reason. It was different here then.

We waited a little while, and then I saw my grandmother and my aunt and my sister come, and they were all bloody. And my grandmother and my aunt said, "Put out the fire. Close up the house, because we're going."

"Why?"

"Because they shot your mother. They went to the house and shot us. Close up."

I don't remember if I closed up or not. We left. We went to sleep up at Javier Vazquez' house. His wife was alive then, and we went there to sleep. And then I asked my grandmother, "Where is my mother?"

"They shot your mother."

"And where is my little brother?"

"We don't know. We would have brought the baby, but they didn't let us. They didn't let us bring the baby boy. They have him. He was left behind with your mother. I couldn't figure out how to bring him."

So then we couldn't go right away to see him because they wouldn't let us. I wanted us to go, and we couldn't.

Explaining the Massacre

Nacho came up with his own understanding of the events that led to the massacre, which he attributed to a quarrel that developed within the UCI over the gun his father-in-law had used to kill Clemencia's disrespectful suitor. He began by describing Clemencia and Eugenia as hotheads, or tahuel cihuameh, a term that many Nahuat used to describe the women in their families. Clemencia and Eugenia were angry over the death of their brother, also called "Nacho," who died when his companions killed him for his father's famous gun.

Well, first of all, those sisters-in-law were hotheads. Did you know Clemencia and Eugenia? Florentino? They were all hotheads. The UCIs killed my brother-in-law "Nacho." His same companions! And "Nacho" carried a gun that belonged to his father. But they got drunk together, and they took the gun from him after they killed him. That's how it was. Then these sisters-in-law, they were very fierce, they went to tell those men something strong like this: "You killed 'Nacho.' Just as you killed him, so you'll die."

Because they had killed their brother. So then the killers got angry about that. For that reason, the day came, they went to see them, and they killed them.

It is possible that the UCIs who killed their companion for a gun feared that Clemencia and Eugenia would use witchcraft to get back at them. Unlike the Azande, the Nahuat do not make a sharp distinction between a sorcerer, who "practices rites with bad medicine," and a witch, who "performs no rite, utters no spell, and possesses no medicine."[12] The Nahuat apply the word nahual to anyone, man or woman, who can do harm to another by practicing a rite.[13]

The fear of the power of witches is palpable in Huitzilan, and, perhaps for that reason, unscrupulous mestizos have tried to extort livestock from the Nahuat by threatening to kill loved ones with evil rites. Thus, there is a possibility that the Nahuat in the UCI, who had fought with and killed Victoria's brother over a famed pistol, might have feared that Clemencia and Eugenia would consult with a nahual or perhaps perform malevolent rites against them. During the interviews between 2003 and 2005, several mestizos and Nahuat brought up witchcraft killings, although they interpreted them in different ways. Mestizos tended to blame the Nahuat in the UCI for killing men and particularly women for being witches (brujos or brujas).

There was one celebrated case of the murder of a Nahuat woman, Erminia, which serves as an example. Erminia was a widow with grown children who had served as a mayordoma, or sponsor of a saint's celebration, during the 1970s before the arrival of the UCI in Huitzilan. No Nahuat I spoke to then thought it worthy of comment that she, a woman, had assumed this responsibility, although all other mayordomos I had known between 1968 and 1978 were men. Erminia, however, died a violent death during the height of the violence following the chopping down of the Talcuaco milpa. The Nahuat I spoke to took issue with the view of some mestizos who pointed to her death as an example of UCI savagery. One Nahuat said that Erminia was drinking in a store at the southern end of town with the Nahuat town hall president, who allegedly was in league with Coyote, and his policemen. There was an argument, and Erminia allegedly said to one of the men drinking with her in the store: "So you'll know, so you'll see I can really do it, you won't see the sunrise tomorrow." She was alluding to her power to kill with witchcraft. She left the drinking party, and the men she threatened agreed among themselves to kill her, and they did.

The Nahuat talked about another case, a man who was a drunk. His wife went to the same town hall president and told him that her husband intended to kill him and his companions, presumably by witchcraft. The wife later informed the president that her husband was getting drunk and she had left him inside the house so they could go in and kill him. The third case involved the murder of a man who had the reputation of saying elaborate prayers at rituals but probably was not a nahual. The Nahuat returning from exile killed him as the Antorcha were driving the

UCI out of Huitzilan. These cases are reason to conclude that the fear of witchcraft had reached a high level at the time Victoria died and may have been part of the motivation for the massacre.

The massacre of Victoria and her family represented for Nacho the complete collapse of the Nahuat moral order, based on love and respect. Chapter 5 will turn to the one story in his repertoire that he said best represents this collapse at that time in Huitzilan's history. That story describes a world in which there are no love, respect, and human goodness and where the bigger and stronger try to devour those who are weaker. Nacho used that story to explain how and why the conflict in Huitzilan arose because men acted on strong and disruptive emotions.

CHAPTER 5

"Rabbit and Coyote"

Nacho selected the very popular folktale "Rabbit and Coyote"[1] as the story in his repertoire that best represents the behavior of the Nahuat in the UCI who killed Victoria and threatened to kill him. For Nacho, this story describes a world in which there are no love and respect. Like the Balinese cockfight described by Geertz,[2] it reveals what the Nahuat are like when they lose their culture. However, the story and Nacho's exegesis also reveal how he was able to reconcile the near-complete breakdown in the social order and in respect with the code of conduct he had learned growing up in Calyecapan.

"Rabbit and Coyote" was the most popular folktale during my earlier fieldwork and continues to have enormous popularity today. I recorded a variant from Antonio Veracruz in 1973 and heard countless others from different narrators between 1973 and 1978. The main characters are: an old woman who has a flower garden; Rabbit, who eats her flowers; and Coyote, who tries to eat Rabbit. The story represents Huitzilan from a Nahuat man's point of view and expresses a broad range of problems in the social structure experienced or witnessed by the many who tell it. The old woman appears to be a Nahuat woman who cultivates her garden of flowers, the symbols of her fertility. Her identity as a Nahuat woman is apparent because narrators frequently call her "lamatzin," a word that means precious turkey and the term husbands use to address and refer to their wives. The reciprocal term women use for men is "huehhuecho," or old tom turkey. Rabbit, the smaller of the two animals, eats vegetables but no meat and is like the Nahuat, who describe themselves in stories as eating corn. Coyote, who hungers for turkey and chicken meat and tries to eat Rabbit, is like the mestizos, who hunger for land and pose a threat to the Nahuat, who need land to grow their food.

Like many trickster tales, "Rabbit and Coyote" is filled with violence, and before 1977 it may have expressed the aggressive fantasies of the Nahuat, who, in many ways, had been under the thumb of the mestizos since at least the time of General Gabriel Barrios, the cacique whose dominion was the northern sierra of Puebla from 1917 to 1930.[3] I mentioned earlier that Gabriel Barrios had established his position in Huitzilan by appointing as his local representatives the oldest of the three Tetela brothers, as well as Victoria's mestizo grandfather, a descendant of Juana Gutierrez, who was the "original" owner of Talcuaco and Taltempan. Gabriel Barrios also had a son with the sister of the three Tetela brothers, and that son became a Puebla state representative.

Since the days of Gabriel Barrios's political dominion, mestizos in Huitzilan had controlled the economy and the town hall government. They left the church to the Nahuat. They controlled the economy by owning most of the land, by having the largest stores, and by owning most of the pack animals used to ship goods in and out of Huitzilan. They had a heavy hand in naming the slate of candidates to serve in the administrative and judicial branches of the town hall government. From the point of view of many Nahuat, they were the "rich ones," or "ricos," who offered them work on the estates they had carved out from what once was Nahuat land. The Nahuat brought up many cases of ancestors who owned land that passed to mestizos who had provided them with alcohol, extended credit in stores, and then demanded payment in land.

The appearance of the UCI in 1977 and the ensuing conflict dislodged the mestizos from their control of the town hall and caused a shift in Nacho's interpretation of this story. Rake, the son of the oldest of the three Tetela brothers, had resigned from the presidency soon after taking office in February 1979, leaving only Nahuat officials in the town hall. Then the UCI killed the Nahuat who took Rake's place and who was allegedly in league with Coyote. The UCI also killed his successor, another Nahuat who had served as Agente de Ministerio Público, and then the UCI became an armed band that roamed Huitzilan pretty much at will. The leaders of the Antorcha Campesina came from outside the community, and, after driving the UCI out of Huitzilan, they took over the town hall in 1984 and have maintained control of it through 2004. All of these changes involved violence, which is one of the reasons that Nacho selected a story with several violent episodes to represent the history of his community from 1977 to 2004. Huitzilan had become a place without love, respect, and compassion, as Nahuat in the UCI turned against other

Nahuat, and "Rabbit and Coyote" also describes an amoral world. In that world, the Nahuat had to use their wits when dealing with the UCI, just as in the story Rabbit must use his wits to escape from Coyote.

An English translation of a version of "Rabbit and Coyote" recounted by Nacho in 2004 appears first, followed by my interpretation of how the story represents the problems in Huitzilan's social structure before 1977. There follows Nacho's interpretation of the meaning this tale has in describing the breakdown of the love, respect, and compassion that he felt should prevail in a marriage, a family, and a community.

NACHO'S "RABBIT AND COYOTE"

The one who told me the story said that one time there was a woman who had a garden. She planted a lot of flowers. And every day that little rabbit came to eat the flowers. So the old woman wondered, "Well, these flowers, where are they going? An animal is eating all of them."

Early in the morning she saw the animal had finished more flowers. He was eating them. He was eating them. So she spied on the rabbit eating. As for what the old woman did, the old woman was smart. She wasn't stupid. She looked for clean wax and she made a doll. And she placed it among the flowers. The rabbit came out of his hole and spoke to the doll: "What are you doing here?"

The doll didn't answer him. Because it was a doll.

Rabbit said, "This is my dinner I eat here. I come to eat. I didn't come to eat my own blood."

That's how he spoke to it, and it didn't answer him.

Rabbit said, "Answer me! What do you say for yourself? You're keeping me from my food. It doesn't answer me," said Rabbit. "If you don't tell me who you are, I'm going to hit you."

He hit it with one hand. His hand got stuck.

"It grabbed me. If you don't let go of me, I'm going to hit you again," said Rabbit.

And yes. He hit it again. His other hand got stuck.

"It grabbed my other hand!" Rabbit exclaimed. "Let go of me! And if you don't, I'm going to give you a kick."

As for what the rabbit did, he drove his foot into the doll. His foot got stuck.

"And why did you grab my foot? Let go of me. I gave you just one kick, and you'll see when I give you another one."

Rabbit gave it another one. His other foot got stuck. It got stuck because the wax was sticky and because Rabbit was small. The next morning the old woman went out again. She saw Rabbit hanging on the wax doll.

"*Darn Rabbit, you ate my flowers. Now you have to pay me.*"

She grabbed him and put him in a basket. She closed the basket and she told him she was going to put water on to boil. She was going to boil him in hot water. And Coyote arrived. Coyote knew where Rabbit was.

"*I'm going to eat you,*" *Coyote told Rabbit.*

"*Don't eat me.*"

"*Yes, I'm going to eat you. I'm very hungry.*"

"*Don't eat me. Someone is coming right now to give me word [about a fiesta]. Someone is going to give me some chicken meat, and I can't eat it. You eat it.*"

"*Really?*"

"*Yes. Someone is coming right now to take me out of here. Someone is going to make a fiesta, and I can't eat meat. Get in here, and I'll go away, and you'll see.*"

Coyote was stupid. He was very big but he was stupid. So then he got into the basket. And Rabbit left. And then the old woman came. She said she was going to put water on to boil. The old woman came back.

"*It's my Rabbit. Now you'll pay me for my flowers.*"

She opened the basket. Coyote came out from inside. Coyote saw the old woman's legs rising above him. Coyote fled. And he went looking for Rabbit.

"*Where is Rabbit?*"

Coyote was angry because Rabbit had tricked him. So he went looking for him. Coyote went looking for him until he found him in one of those green places. You call it a lake. Coyote found Rabbit up on the shore. And at that moment there was a full moon. Rabbit had been there a long time. He was looking down.

"*So you're here, that's the way it'll be, yes, I'm going to eat you,*" *said Coyote. "You tricked me. You said they were going to feed you. Where? She was about to kill me. Now I'm going to eat you.*"

Rabbit pleaded, "Don't eat me. I don't eat cheese. I can't go get that cheese over there. You can, so run. It'll be good. Show us how it's done. You eat it. Me? Don't eat me!"

Coyote asked, "Really?"

Rabbit said, "Yes. That's cheese. I can't get it."

As for what Coyote did, well it was a little bit of something far away, and so he tried to grab it with one of his paws, and he couldn't grab it.

Rabbit fled. He fled. And so Coyote went looking for him and he went look-ing for him. He found him again. He found him at the base of a mountain. It was cloudy. There were clouds. The clouds were moving. And Coyote found Rabbit with his back against the mountain. He was holding it up.

"Yes, now I'm going to eat you. You tricked me back there."

"Don't eat me. Look, this mountain is going to fall. Help me hold it up. Look! If someone doesn't hold up the mountain, it's really going to fall down. The clouds are hitting the mountain."

So Coyote backed himself up against the mountain.

"Push hard, and I'll take a good look. I'm going to see if it'll crush us."

Rabbit fled while Coyote went to prop it up. That's how it was. Coyote walked around looking for him until the day came when he found him in a fallow field.

Coyote said to him, "Now I'm going to eat you for sure. You tricked me in three places. I'm going to eat you right now."

"Don't eat me," said Rabbit. "Right now someone is going to make a fiesta. Someone is going to make a big fiesta, and you can dance and you can get drunk, and as for me and drinking, I can't drink. Go into the middle of that . . . burned place and go over there. And you'll see. You'll hear when the rockets [announcing the fiesta] start exploding."

Coyote believed him. He went over and sat in the middle of that fallow field. The storyteller said Rabbit circled around that burned place. Rabbit set the place on fire. The fire started burning. Coyote stayed in the middle. It started exploding. But who said a rocket had exploded? And it finished Coyote and burned him all up. There it ended.

The main oppositions among the three characters capture some of the important problems in Nahuat social structure prior to the arrival of the UCI. Rabbit tries to eat the old Nahuat woman's flowers, the old woman catches and tries to eat Rabbit, Coyote tries to eat Rabbit, and Rabbit lures Coyote to his death with the ruse of an approaching fiesta. The opposition between the old Nahuat woman and Rabbit al-ludes to the tension in gender relations between a woman and her disre-spectful sons and grandsons. An angry woman (tahuel cihuat) wielding a switch (cuauhpitzac) can hand out harsh punishment. She is also like the mother-in-law who can be a harsh critic of her daughters-in-law. She is a pivotal figure in her patrilineal extended family, much as is a woman in the matrilineal families of other societies.[4]

The opposition between Rabbit and Coyote represents the tensions between Nahuat and mestizos, which was the focus in many stories circulating in oral tradition during my earlier fieldwork. The story seems to be what Scott had in mind when he described trickster tales as "the veiled cultural resistance of subordinate groups."[5] There are many parallels between "Rabbit and Coyote" and the African American slave stories of "Brer Rabbit."[6] Rabbit, the smaller animal, can never win in a direct confrontation with the bigger Coyote, much as the Nahuat can never directly oppose the power of the mestizos. It is a veiled form of cultural resistance because as an animal tale it "ostensibly appears to have nothing to do with human society."[7] Scott reminds us that it does,[8] and the dead giveaway is that the Nahuat word for a mestizo is coyote, or "coyot."

The parallels the Nahuat see between the character Coyote and mestizos are apparent from Nacho's account of the experience of Padre Martin, a Nahuat from Huitzilan who became a priest and celebrated his first mass in that community after the UCIs had died in clashes with a superior government force or fled from the community. Nacho recalled the ways in which the mestizo I have called Coyote was greedy even for Padre Martin's land.

"I remember Coyote was not a good man, because, well, I'm not the only one who says it, because everyone mentions how he tricked them. No less than Padre Martin had a plot of land here in Metzancuauhtah [Foot of the Forest].

"Padre Martin said: 'One time they spoke to me. The old man told me to sell him the land, sell it to him because they were all around my plot. My piece was in the middle of his land. So then he told me to sell the land, sell it to him. He did not win me over. I did not want to sell it. The old woman came. She told me again to sell him the land. I didn't want to. They all came to see it, the old woman, Coyote's wife, and Coyote's son. Again, he tried hard to get me to sell the land because it was a gap in the middle of their lands. He'd take it from me. But I didn't want to sell it. Again Coyote's daughter came. She said for me to sell the land. And I didn't want to. They got angry.'

"He was tricky when he coveted land."

"Rabbit and Coyote" Today

In his exegesis in 2004, Nacho shifted the emphasis from Coyote as a mestizo to Coyote as the UCI to fit the historical changes that had taken place in his community. Now Nacho characterized Coyote as a menacing tecuani, or "wild beast."[9] In his explanation of the story's new meaning, Nacho revealed how he reconciled the violent events that had taken place in Huitzilan with his idealized code of conduct based on human goodness. Nacho used the story to explain evil by pointing out that strong emotions drive the cycles of history, in which one group of men uses force to dominate other men. Those strong emotions are what prevent men and women from living with love, respect, and compassion.

Nacho's Explanation

"For me, well, Rabbit is very small, and Coyote is big. He's a human eater. But although he is a big human eater and Rabbit is small, the small one looks for a way to vanquish the big one. So then he looks for a way to win. One also knows how the UCIs came in, they felt like big human eaters, they had guns, but there is also one who, even if he does not have anything, looks for a way to win. Also, that story is wise about the way people are. It represents humanity because there is a great deal of everything in the world. There is conflict, there is rage, and with that, I think our ancestors made these stories because they knew how to do things, how to think."

At one point in his interpretation, he referred to the UCI as great big human eaters, or hueihuei tecuani, alluding to the common criticism "to act big," which refers to being selfish, refusing to work with others, and acting superior. He had noted earlier that Wrath accused him of acting big, apparently because he had refused to work with the UCI. Of course, Nacho's shift in the meaning of the character of Coyote is understandable if one considers that the UCI killed Victoria, and that the mestizos lost control over the town hall in 1984. Shifting what Coyote symbolizes from a mestizo to the UCI is an expression of the Nahuat cyclical conception of time, according to which no structure is permanent, just as Nacho explained that no group will remain dominant forever. The Nahuat cycle of history has something in common with the cycle of nature—the corn plant and the diurnal and annual cycles of the sun—according to which the Nahuat constructed their quadrilateral view of the universe. The notion of history as cyclical has ancient antecedents, as Michel Graulich pointed out in his interpretation of the sixteenth-century Nahua myths.[10] According to Graulich, the ancient Nahuas represented history as a series of cycles in which vigorous but uncultured hunters and gatherers take over sedentary agriculturalists.

Nacho did not attribute the cycle of history in Huitzilan to a supernatural cause, but instead traced the origin of violent events directly "back to man."[11] He talked about the role of human emotions that include fear (mauhcayot), anger (cualayot), and obsessive love as desire (tazohtaliz) to explain the events in Huitzilan's history. In an interview that took place a year later,[12] he said: "Fear got ahold of us. It was fear. Fear killed us. We didn't know what to do. We just got angry with each other." In his story, he had told how people like Wrath and Dog changed as fear got hold of them. About Wrath, Nacho said: "He used to be a good person. He was respectful." Nacho explained: "Anger makes the inside of our hearts cold." Wrath changed, he said, because "People from far away came. They put ideas into his head. And having a gun always changes one's thinking. If you have a gun, you'll think you're very big."

Nacho said that anger was there before the UCI arrived in Huitzilan, but "one couldn't do anything with it." I asked about the source of the anger, and Nacho referred to the problems Wrath and Dog had with Wolf over women. Regarding Wrath, he said: "Maybe it was because his wife left him. Perhaps her brother, who was Wolf, fought with him. And Dog, because of that same Wolf, they got angry over that woman. At that time, Dog didn't have anyone to help him. He didn't have anyone with whom he could become brave. He couldn't do anything. After he had a gun, the anger came out and he looked for someone to fight."

After describing "Rabbit and Coyote" as a story about what happened to the Nahuat when they lost their culture, he concluded his three days of narration by telling me about rituals that could restore the culture they lost. Those rituals have as their purpose to tie people together with bonds of human goodness, and those rituals are the topic of Chapter 6.

CHAPTER 6

Human Goodness

The Nahuat word for human goodness is cualtacayot, which is a combination of "cual-li," or "something good," and "tacayot," or "humanity."[1] After Nacho had finished telling me his story, he decided to describe how the Nahuat could reach back into their culture and spread human goodness through their rituals to restore the respect, or icnoyot, that was lost during the violence that cost Victoria her life. He chose for his example the rituals of godparenthood that are part of baptism and marriage. Among the Nahuat of his community, it was common practice for the godparents of marriage to become the godparents of baptism for the married couple's children. Baptism and marriage rituals are similar because the main participants wear a flower necklace, called a xochicozcat, and carry a flower tree, called a xochicuahuit.

The flower tree is an adornment that may originally have represented the tree of Tamoanchan, depicted in the sixteenth-century Codex Telleriano Remensis.[2] López Austin explained that Tamoanchan is a mythical as well as historical place located variously near the Moon on the top of a high mountain, among the volcanoes surrounding the Valley of Mexico, and in the ancient city of Teotihuacan.[3] Michel Graulich explained the meaning of Tamoanchan as a mythical place by observing that in this realm resided the God of Two, or the God of Duality, Ometeotl, who had both a masculine and a feminine aspect.[4] The masculine aspect was Lord of the Flesh, or Tonacateuctli, and the feminine aspect was Lady of the Flesh, or Tonacacihuatl. The God of Two had the power to procreate other gods who did the work of creation. One of the goddesses was Quetzal Flower, or Xochiquetzal, who usurped the power of procreation by cutting flowers and branches from a forbidden tree in Tamoanchan.

Woman with xochicuahuit

The tree shattered, causing a rupture between the celestial and the earthly realms. Xochiquetzal's act of cutting the flower and breaking the branch infuriated the God of Two, who banished her to earth.[5] Xochiquetzal gave birth to Cinteotl, the god of corn, from whose body emerged edible plants.[6] López Austin interpreted the flower tree as the device that both separated and connected the celestial and earthly realms. He called the flower trees "posts" preventing the recombination "of the masculine and the feminine halves of the universe as well as pathways for the gods to travel between them."[7]

That tree probably became the flower tree used in contemporary rituals in different parts of the northern sierra of Puebla, including Huitzilan. López Austin mentioned a number of reports by anthropologists who have described flower trees and their meaning in different communities in the general vicinity of Huitzilan. Contemporary Nahuas in one community say that the tree stands in the water that is the heart of the earth,[8] and in another they regard the trees as supporting the four corners of the earth.[9] The Otomis consider the tree a symbol of ritual energy.[10] The Totonacs regard it as the passageway for souls and divinities, wind and water, traveling between the moist, dark feminine earth and the dry, bright masculine space above the earth.[11]

The Flower Tree in Huitzilan

The original creation myth of Xochiquetzal cutting the flower tree in Tamoanchan has long disappeared from the consciousness of the Nahuat in Huitzilan and has become part of the biblical story of "Adam and Eve." In Huitzilan, Nahuat narrators of that biblical story say the tree ascended to heaven after the first couple ate the forbidden fruit.[12] Nacho declared that the three prongs of the flower tree adornment in Huitzilan represent the Trinity: God the Father, God the Son, and God the Holy Spirit. At the time of my earlier fieldwork (1968–1978), the Nahuat spent a great deal of money on rituals involving use of the flower tree, some selling all of the land they inherited from their parents. When the price of coffee rose, one would hear, in many corners of the Huitzilan valley, rockets announcing that there was a flower tree ritual open to anyone who wished to attend. When I returned to Huitzilan in 2003, many Nahuat told me that they no longer celebrate their weddings with the flower tree. However, the town hall authorities have incorporated that tree into their civil ceremonies, aimed ostensibly at recognizing the importance of Nahuat culture in Huitzilan.

Some Nahuat do not approve of the town hall using the flower tree in civil ceremonies, because it has a very specific meaning, which Nacho explained on the third day of his narration. Nacho described what the flower tree meant to him, saying that the purpose of the flower tree celebration is to create human goodness, or cualtacayot, among the participants. The essence of human goodness is love, or tazohtaliz, respect, or icnoyot, and compassion, or teicneliliz, which are supposed to prevail in all aspects of human relations. His explanation made a great deal of

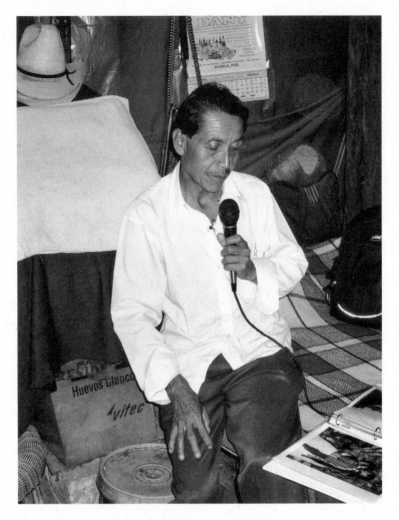

Nacho talking about xochicuahuit rituals

sense to me based on my observations of many betrothal, baptismal, and particularly wedding celebrations during my earlier fieldwork.

For the connection between love and the flower tree, I now turn to what Nacho wanted to tell me and wanted me to record. He began by mentioning a book I had published in Spanish that included a description, but not an interpretation, of the rituals with the flower tree adornment that he believed spread human goodness, or caultacayot.[13] He had lost the book during the chaos of the anger and had forgotten about the description of the rituals.

Nacho: "I do not know if you have this in your book, if you wrote it down, you probably do because you wrote a long time ago, but we remember a lot of customs. We remember many customs. When someone cares for and feeds a child and sprinkles water in baptism, we remember that it's called purifying a godchild. One sprinkles water to purify someone. It means that one purifies someone so he or she will be free. And then that's when one wears a flower necklace [xochicozcat]. Do you remember?"

Jim: "I sure do."

Nacho: "One wears a flower necklace [xochicozcat]. The necklace has flowers and bread. And one also gives a flower tree [xochicuahuit] with three pieces of wood. It has flowers and bread. We say it means—I don't know if it's good or bad—that the flower necklace fastens people together. We see the necklace as making a circle. One realizes there is a circle and flowers. Why? Because our god is all around us. God is all around us. And we are inside. We are inside. So then I want to begin doing this recording so that we do not forget about this custom. It is a very good idea. It is very precious. Then one also knows when one of our compadres puts that flower around his compadre's neck, that means we are fastened together so that we never forget, so that the goodness will never end. So that it never comes unfastened. So that they observe us with good thoughts. If my godchild, he speaks to me, bringing me that flower, to get married, then it means that those godchildren never forget their love. May they always have it inside their house. Because when one of my compadres comes to see that flower, it means we are fastened to each other. So we won't become unfastened. So we don't criticize each other. So we don't mistreat each other. So we don't get angry with each other. Because with that flower—how shall I put it?—we are fastened to our godfather. And that circle is God surrounding us. Surrounding us. And we are inside. That's how it is. And that flower tree, when our compadre gives it to us, it has three sticks. Three sticks of wood also mean our god the father, our god his son, and our god the Holy Spirit. That's what it is. And it has flowers. The flowers are the same. They also represent saintly God. And the bread, since one puts a certain amount of bread, all white bread, a 'bolillo,' it also means so that one will always have a piece of bread. So one won't see there is nothing. So one won't go hungry. That's what it means to us to give that flower. Those customs are very beautiful. They are very pure. Such as the custom of feeding the compadre, he sits at the table or on the ground, because they did not used to have tables then, and they serve the compadre who views the tortillas. He views the dinner. They bring him the turkey, turkey meat, because that's what they bring, as a gift to him. So then they do not show it to him when it is alive, but they view it as it is adorned in a basket or on big dishes. Then they view the tor-

Wedding banquet

tillas. There might be two baskets or two gourds, one of those big gourds. So then the comadre will give one of those tortillas. She'll bring an end to viewing the tortillas. When they eat, first the comadre will begin. She'll take a tortilla, and each one of them will give one. All of her companions will exchange one. They begin soaking the tortillas in the meat sauce. The comadre, she gives to her compadre, and then another comadre gives to her compadre. Or her godchild soaks his tortilla that way to mean that they have that big love. It's very pure because she'll eat what I'll eat. That is a very beautiful thing. And we remember so we might end that way. One also exchanges drinks, like aguardiente, the compadre gives one bottle, one bottle comes from the comadre, another bottle from another one, another bottle from another one. Each one has a bottle with a flower around its neck. It too wears a flower necklace. And each one has a package of cigarettes. So then once they stop eating, they begin exchanging drinks, they divide the drinks into equal portions. Once they conclude, then our comadre picks up a flower tree and a flower necklace, she takes hold of that flower tree and begins to dance. All of her comadres line up to wait their turn. They're all women. They dance until finished, and the compadre gets up. He starts dancing. All the men dance. It ends there. Everyone finishes. They do a tune called 'the dance of four [nanahui].' Do you remember it?"

Nanahui

Jim: "Yes."

Nacho: "Then those four do 'the dance of four' with an incense carrier, or 'tapopoxhuiqueh.' Then that incense carrier, she places the bride and groom and the godmother and godfather of marriage in the four corners or in a square that makes me recall the four points of the earth. They are the four points of the earth. We call them the four cardinal points. And our god is in the center. So then I would not like to lose this. Let there be adorning rituals. And that incense carrier [tapopoxhuiqueh], when she dances, she starts to fasten them all together. She fastens them all together. So then that means the celebration is over. They must remain fastened. It doesn't just end after they are fastened together. They are stuck together with God. They fastened themselves together. So then we want them to go adorn so they don't forget. For us, that is our culture."

Huitzilan as Ceremonial Center

At the conclusion of his explanation, Nacho represented Huitzilan as a ceremonial center for the region that includes a number of other Nahuat-speaking communities in the sierra. The ceremonial center he had in mind was different than the ones of pre-Hispanic times, which had sacred spaces organized around pyramids, where priests carried out rituals involving human sacrifice. Rather, he described Huitzilan as having highly efficacious rituals involving the use of the flower tree, or xochicuahuit. Moreover, he added that, among the communities he knew personally in the northern sierra of Puebla, only in Huitzilan can one find the flower tree.[14] The communities missing the flower tree that Nacho specifically mentioned were Pahuatla, Huahuaxtla, and Xochitlán, which circle Huitzilan in a rotation from south to east to north. He did not mention the Totonac community of Zongozotla to the west.[15] Nacho made clear that Huitzilan is a ceremonial center for this region precisely because only the Nahuat in his community use the flower tree [xochicuahuit] in their rituals. He did not come right out and say that Huitzilan was a ceremonial center, because to do so would be to act big, or hueichihua. Instead, he repeated a conversation with a friend whom he quoted as saying: "We go to Pahuatla, we go to Huahuaxtla, we go to Xochitlán, and they ask us how we do our rituals with the flower tree. Other towns do not do them that way. They give the flower necklace but not the flower tree like we do. And they dance differently. So then they ask us, 'How do you do it?' They very much want to do what we do. They say, 'Well you can, and we don't know how. Tell us, tell us so we'll go tell others how. Because we don't know.'"

Spreading Human Goodness with the Flower Tree

Nacho's description of the ceremonies involving the flower necklace and the flower tree reveals that the rituals represent the spatial arrangement of the universe, and are mysteriously efficacious in fastening people together, particularly men and women. He specifically mentioned that the dance of four, or nanahui, represents the four cardinal directions. As mentioned earlier, the Nahuat orient themselves precisely in space according to their quadrilateral view of the universe. Narrators place the action of their stories precisely in space relative to the masculine mountains flanking Huitzilan to the east; the feminine ones to the west; the home of Nanahuatzin, the captain of the rain gods, or "quiyauhteomeh," to the north; and the homeland of the mestizos to the south. As this list reveals, the Nahuat attach meaning to the four cardinal directions according to their geocentric conception of the universe and their historical experiences.[16]

Regarding the efficacy of the rituals in fastening people together, Nacho invoked the image of sewing a garment. He used the verb "tzicoā," meaning "to stick, fasten one thing to another,"[17] and emphasized through verbal repetition the efficacy of this Nahuat ritual of fastening. He employed the verb "to fasten" (tzicoā) five times when describing the incense carrier's role. It is a common practice to give emphasis by repeating a phrase, a word, or a syllable within a word. He continued his use of sewing imagery by employing the verb "tohtoma," meaning "to undress, to unfasten, to loosen something,"[18] to refer to the breakdown of respect like what occurred during the rage, or cualayot. What can be fastened also can come unfastened, as Nacho experienced during the years leading up to and following Victoria's death.

The creation of ties between men and women is evident in the food exchanged across gender lines. Nacho described a food exchange that involves the principal eight participants at a ceremony in honor of the godparents of marriage: the bride, the groom, the bride's mother and father, the groom's mother and father, and the godparents. The eight observe the banquet as an act of respect for the seriousness of the occasion, and then they carry out an exchange of tortillas across gender lines. In every case, a woman initiates the exchange by taking a tortilla from one of the baskets or large gourds, dipping it in the sauce from her banquet bowl, and giving the tortilla to her compadre. Nacho said about this exchange: "The comadre, she gives to her compadre, and then another comadre gives to her compadre. Or her godchild soaks the tortilla that way to mean they have a big love. It's very pure because she'll eat what I'll eat. Then that is a very beautiful thing."

Women as Fasteners

The use of sewing imagery in Nacho's narrative reminds one of the quote from a New Caledonian native that appeared in Marcel Mauss's *The Gift:* "Our feasts are the movement of the needle which sews together the parts of our reed roofs, making them a single roof, one single word."[19] Among the Nahuat, the images of sewing and food also remind one of women's work; women sew garments and they prepare daily meals as well as wedding banquets. Moreover, a woman is always the tapopoxhuiqueh, or incense carrier, as well as the intermediary, or "cihuatanqueh," whom the boy's family chooses to represent them to the girl's family when initiating marriage negotiations. Nacho's description of the role of women in the ritual for spreading human goodness, or cualtacayot, led to a consideration of the place of the woman in the circle that Nacho said the flower necklace, or xochicozcat, represented. There is a parallel between the importance of women in rituals that spread human goodness and some aspects of the place of the feminine in ancient Nahua thought. Nacho placed the feminine in the center of his universe and emphasized the connection between masculine and feminine.[20]

In the following chapters, I shall draw on my earlier fieldwork to reveal how he came to develop his ideas about women and his meanings of love with respect. Chapter 7 will focus on Nacho's mother and his experiences growing up in a large extended family household in Calyecapan.

CHAPTER 7

Nahueh

Nacho was twenty-four, single, and living with his widowed mother, his two older brothers, their wives, and their children in Calyecapan when I arrived in Huitzilan in 1968. The members of his large extended family lived in two wooden houses. In the larger of the two lived Nacho, his mother, his oldest brother, Miguel, Miguel's wife, María Agustina Ayance, and their children. In the smaller lived Nicolás, his wife, María Gabriela Sánchez, and their children. Nacho would beckon me to enter his house, a cavernous and dark space with a cleanly swept earthen floor, an altar with images of saints, and neat rows of dried corn in its husks piled behind the altar. He would offer me a small bench, and his mother, Gabriela, a thin woman of sixty-five, would serve me a cup of coffee sweetened with brown sugar. If it was mealtime, Gabriela would kneel at her grinding stone, plop on handfuls of dried corn boiled in lime, grind the corn to a very fine dough, slap out tortillas, and place them on a clay griddle supported by three hearthstones. She would skillfully control the flame under the griddle by inserting sticks of firewood between the hearthstones so the tortillas would puff up with air and cook but not burn.

Nahueh as Kin Term

Nacho referred to and addressed his mother as "nahueh," a term that has many meanings, depending on the context. I once heard him use it when, with warmth in his voice, he asked his young niece, "What are you doing, nahueh?"[1] She replied with alacrity, telling Nacho all of the things she had done playing with her siblings and cousins in the clearing next to the house. Nacho liked children and frequently spoke to them with respect, or icnoyot, and affection. Nacho also used the term nahueh when referring to Blancaflor, or White Flower, the main character with magical powers in the popular folktale mentioned earlier. These various meanings of nahueh are among the components in his image of women, acquired growing up in Calyecapan.

Nacho told the story of "Blancaflor" in 1970 when still living with his mother and older brothers, and his particular way of describing the main female character reveals something about his image of women as he was poised to marry Victoria a few months later. In his story, Blancaflor helped her lover, Juan, perform incredible tasks and flee from her father. They reach Juan's home, where he forgets about her and is about to marry another woman. He asks Blancaflor to prepare the wedding banquet because he has heard she can produce large meals very quickly, as if by magic. Blancaflor makes two dolls, one in her image and the other resembling Juan, and she has the dolls talk to each other during the wedding. Every time Blancaflor reminds Juan of a task she performed for him, she strikes him with her shawl, and when she strikes him the fourth time, he responds by saying: "Oh, nahueh, don't hit me . . . I'm remembering."[2] The number four is significant because it represents completeness, standing for the four points in the Nahuas' quadrilateral view of the universe. The Nahuat represent that universe in the climactic wedding dance called "the dance of four," or nanahui. The four participants are the bride and groom and godmother and godfather. An incense carrier, usually the woman who arranged the marriage between the two families, weaves the participants into bonds of human goodness, or cualtacayot, with incense.

Nahueh is, thus, a respectful term of reference and address for mother, an affectionate term of address for a young girl who will become a mother, and a term a man would apply to a woman who is or will become his wife. The use of the term nahueh for a woman who has the power of procreation and the ability to produce vast quantities of food quickly and with little apparent effort, as if by magic, fits the actual contribution of women to the Nahuat household. Women give birth to children whose labor will eventually produce corn that goes into the granary and will then turn that corn into tortillas. As a component of Nacho's image of woman, nahueh represents feminine powers of creation.

Town and Cihuatepet

The Meaning of Nahueh

As our conversation came to a close in 2004, Nacho and I talked about the location of women in the sacred space he represented by the flower necklace, or xochicozcat. He had said that the necklace makes a circle to represent God surrounding us. I began by bringing up the meaning of the term nahueh, the term of reference and address for mother. The term nahueh is related to other words, including "nahuauhtequi," which means "to hug oneself, to embrace someone," and "nahuaqueh," which translates as "the one that is close to all things, god."[3] It occurred to me that perhaps God and nahueh were one in the same person, and I wondered if Nacho thought of nahueh as a goddess. He had not thought of the meaning of nahueh in those terms, but then he considered the ways in which God and woman are associated. He said: "Our god, he stays next to woman so that she makes children. Our god worries so we don't suffer. Our mother is the same. She is always worrying about us."

After Nacho and I talked about the meaning of nahueh, we climbed up the mountains bounding Huitzilan to the east, and we turned west to look down at the town in the valley below. I noticed that the church, which marks the center of town, lies at the base of Cihuatepet, or Woman Mountain, precisely at her center. Nacho and I wondered exactly why the church stands where it does, but we both agreed the location was significant. Nacho explained that the center of town is actually between Cihuatepet to the west and the masculine mountain of Tacalot, or Man of Stone, to the east. He said that it was as if the town is cradled between its mother (Cihuatepet) and its father (Tacalot).

Gabriela

The woman who had the greatest influence on Nacho's images of women at this point in his life (1970) was his mother, Gabriela, who was born in Calyecapan. Gabriela married Nacho's father, Alfonso Angel, who was born in Taltzintan, or "Land at the Foot" of the mountains, just below Talcuaco. Gabriela brought her husband to live with her family. At first they lived in a house on her family's land, and then she obtained a house-site of her own in return for taking care of her elderly mother. Her extended family was organized around her brother, Bartolomé Hernández, who was one of the richest Nahuat men in Huitzilan. Nearly all of Bartolomé's land went to his son Domingo. Alfonso brought into the marriage two plots of land, which Gabriela eventually divided among her children. Gabriela gave birth to many children in Calyecapan, four of whom survived into Nacho's lifetime. Nacho saw his father and younger brother die and his older brothers marry. Gabriela strengthened her position by skillfully managing her family relationships. Nacho explained: "She was a good person. Even though some will say she was a hothead. But no. She wasn't. She had her daughters-in-law, and she never fought with them. Because there are mothers-in-law who do fight with their daughters-in-law." Quarrels between mothers and daughters-in-law were one of the most common reasons for why many married sons established their own independent households relatively soon after marriage.

Tazohtaliz as Maternal Love

To gain a fuller picture of how Nacho learned about love from his mother, I asked him in 2004 how he knew that his mother—now deceased—loved him. He said: "Because she was waiting for me with my tortillas. She begged me to eat. If I arrived, she'd bend down to say, 'Eat, while they're hot.' I knew she loved me. Because once she leaves you, she doesn't say, 'Eat.' You'd always arrive, and she'd say, 'Drink coffee. Eat.' If I'd go, she'd say, 'Don't be long. Come soon. Come back soon.' So then one sees she loves you." Nacho was speaking about his mother offering him food after he had separated from her household and was living with Victoria, first next door to her father, and then in Talcez.

There are two things to note about Nacho's description of how he knew his mother loved him. The first is that he connected love with a woman offering him food, which is reminiscent of how he had described Blancaflor as nahueh, as one who had the capacity to cook vast quantities of food quickly and with apparently little effort, as if by magic. The second is that his mother desired that he return to be with her soon. While her request may not strike the reader as unusual, it is worthy of mention because Nacho and other Nahuat frequently represent love as the desire to be near another. One of the most common metaphorical expressions for love concerns looking for another, using the verb "temoa," meaning "to look for someone." Epifania had used this expression to describe how she and her brothers and sister grieved for their mother. She said: "I was very sad and I cried because I wanted to see my mother. My brothers and sister did too. They looked for my mother. We were sad and we cried. What could we do?"

Love and Work

Love and work also have a relationship in Nahua culture; Gabriela worked to make the food she gave Nacho when he visited her. Catherine Good noted that the Guerrero Nahuatl link love and work by saying that those who work together also love each other. Conversely, those who no longer work together cease to love each other. Love and grief also have a connection through work because Guerrero Nahuatl women said that they mourned their dead children for the work they could not perform.[4] Nacho put it this way: "If a person works, one sees that he or she is a good person who works well with one, and one loves the person for it because that person is doing what I would like to do but cannot do by myself." Nacho also expressed how love and work are related by showing compassion (teicneliliz) for those who are members of the same family. He expressed his compassion for his parents by describing how they suffered hardship, or "ihiyohuiah," because they had to work hard while he, Nacho, was a child and could not contribute much to the household labor. He also recalled how the deaths of his father and his younger brothers added to his family's hardship.

> My parents suffered a great deal. They carried loaves of brown sugar with a tumpline to Totutla [seven kilometers from Huitzilan]. And they went to sell things in Zapotitlán [five kilometers distant]. And that's how they supported themselves. I was still a child. I couldn't go, and they couldn't take me. But the day came when I don't know what happened to my father. I was just ten years old. And my father had carried some loaves of brown sugar. I remember that he took a lot of loaves. And that afternoon he went into the temazcal [steam bath]. And that night a chill grabbed him, a big chill. He got a fever. And the next morning, he didn't go to Zapotitlán because he was so sick. Just my brothers Miguel and Nicolás and my mother went to sell. I stayed home, and my father was with my comadre Agustina [Miguel's wife]. She was the one we stayed with. The fever took hold of him again around noon, a big chill grabbed hold of my father, and it was so strong, he couldn't speak. A huge fever grabbed him. And it continued on through that evening, all that evening, and the next morning he didn't wake up. He had died. Like I told you, I was a child then. I couldn't do anything.

Nacho remembered his father as a man who was very devoted to the Catholic Church. "My father taught us to be very good Catholics. He taught us about religion. He always took us to church. He took us to church every time there was a mass."

Nacho also spoke of his brother's death not long after his father had died. "But then my brother Victor got sick. And we say that erysipelas grabbed him in the head,[5] and he died. He didn't survive, because there wasn't medicine here then, there weren't any doctors. He died."

Nacho recalled attending school for the first time and then thinking that he would have to quit school and work after his father died.

> I had gone to school when my father was still alive. My mother wasn't going to send me without me going with my cousin.
> I said to my mother, "Let me go to school."
> She said, "No. You'll cry. You'll cry when I get up to go. You'll cry."
> I said, "I won't cry."
> She didn't want me to go. So I put myself in school when my cousin went. But we studied for only one year, we studied in school, and my father started getting sick. Then he suddenly died. So then I said, "I won't go to school anymore because my father is dead. Who will support us?"

My mother kept saying, "No. Go. You're a child. Go learn."

So I went. I finished the first grade in primary school. So I left school, but my mother told me to go back to school again. I studied, I studied until I was thirteen years old. I had scarcely finished the third grade, and I didn't want to go to school because I had to work, and there wasn't anyone to support us. So I started to work. I worked as far away as Zapotitlán, down next to the river. We call it Atentamayan. We worked there planting corn. And I met a teacher, his name was José Nieto, and he used to be a teacher in Zapotitlán. He came over here to teach us.

I met him, and he asked me, "Why don't you go to school?"

I said, "I can't because of work, and we don't have anyone to support us."

He said, "How old are you?"

I said, "Fourteen."

Then he said, "Go talk to Ponciano [Victoria's mestizo grandfather]."

But I never went. I just stayed where I was in the third grade, until I heard there was night school. They taught classes in the evening. I started studying there. I went there a couple of times to learn. I went there to study. Then I was able to go a little more.

Sugarcane and Corn

Nacho described an economy based on sugarcane, corn, and coffee and told how he and his brothers sometimes earned their wages in kernels of corn rather than money.

Meanwhile we worked, we worked in the milpa. We went to work. We planted sugarcane. That was when coffee wasn't worth anything, just a little bit. They planted sugarcane. Well, from then on we went with sugarcane. They expressed the juice. We worked in the sugarcane press [trapiche]. Since it did not belong to us, we went to help whomever it belonged to. And that's the way it was. And when I was a smaller child, my poor mother really suffered. She'd go to make tortillas. She made tortillas for the sugarcane workers. I went with her. She fed me there. And so it was until we went to help my now-deceased uncle, Bartolomé Hernández, with his sugarcane press. It was the one he left to his son Domingo Hernández. I also earned money working with a hoe, but I only earned about one and a half pesos a day or half an almud of corn. And that was all. Day after day we earned half an almud of corn. And if we wanted money, they just gave us the value of half an almud of corn. And that's the way it was. That's how we lived on kernels of corn. And if not, then we made our mother suffer. And we sold wood. We fetched firewood and sold it. And if not, when there were pack animals—there used to be a lot of muleteers—we brought zacate [grass] and sold it. That's how it was. Then afterwards we worked, we worked until I became a man, and my brothers and I, the three of us, started working together. So then we started to have corn. We planted here at Ateno. Corn was more expensive. That's when we didn't suffer anymore for lack of food. We didn't suffer anymore. But as for money, we were suffering because there wasn't any money. When we needed money, we went to work here in Zapotitlán. We looked for a patrón there. We broke ground for planting coffee. We earned our money there. We bought clothes, but only when we earned our money there. When a fiesta came, it was the same thing. Corn also appeared in Zapotitlán. We went there to harvest corn. We harvested in July. We took out the corn to buy something for the fiesta in August. And that's how we lived.

Love versus Work

The theme of suffering hardship by working hard appears in many Nahuat recollections of experience. Sometimes the work and the suffering are so great that they conflict with love, as when, for example, a person who works with others feels exploited, mistreated, or abused. The person who feels mistreated may erupt in anger and accuse others of lacking love. Antonia, a woman I knew well in Huitzilan, recalled feeling that her grandparents did not love her when in such a situation many years earlier. They had her carrying very heavy loads of fruit with a huahcal over very long distances from Huitzilan to and from other communities in the northern sierra of Puebla over rocky roads that cut her bare feet. A huahcal is a wood-and-mesh frame for carrying loads on one's back with a tumpline.

I was around fourteen years old. And they loaded us up with a huahcal of oranges. And then we took it as far as Zacapoaxtla [thirty-two kilometers from Huitzilan]. But we really got tired. And we'd come right back with a load of corn we bought with the oranges. And every week we went, we went to Zacapoaxtla. We'd return every Thursday. They'd cut the oranges, and we'd go to Totutla [seven kilometers away]. From there we'd return from Totutla on Saturday, and they cut oranges, and we'd go to Xochitlán [fifteen kilometers distant]. Then the oranges ended, and it was time for the tiltzapotes [black sapota]. They'd load us with them after they had ripened. And they loaded us up when we were so tired that we cried as we carried the load on the road. It cut up our feet. The rocks cut us. And then, they loaded us with cuauhtzapot [wild sapota]. They treated us like pack animals. They loaded us up. But one time we didn't want to go anymore. We were working in front of the house as they loaded us up to go. We loosened the load. We dropped the load when we were like this little child [pointing to her grandson]. We said, "You work us as if we weren't Christians. You don't love us enough to let us stay near the house." But it wasn't always that way. They gave us work, but they never hit us all the time we were growing up. They never hit me. Not once. My father never hit me and my mother never hit me. And they were hotheads, but neither one hit me, because I did what I was told.

One conclusion from Antonia's testimony is that the Nahuat word for love, or tazohtaliz, as in her remark "You didn't love us" ("Ahmo techtazohtayah"), has a meaning related to but also more than the feeling or experience of "working together." Antonia accused her grandparents of not loving her by not taking into consideration her well-being. Her grandparents, in her view, lacked compassion, or teicneliliz, by asking that she suffer, or ihiyohuia, excessively by transporting heavy loads with her bare feet over rocky roads. Antonia's suffering was so great that she uncharacteristically defied her grandparents by dropping her load of fruit on the ground. Other Nahuat in Antonia's position reacted by refusing to carry out difficult and painful tasks and by separating from parents and setting up their independent households.

Respect

Antonia concluded her anecdote by emphasizing that, other than upon this occasion of her rebellion, she behaved with respect, or icnoyot, toward her parents and grandparents. Respect is the concept in practical religion[6] that is supposed to guide Nahuat behavior. The Nahuat term for respect, icnoyot, has deep historical and cultural antecedents. Alonso de Molina included the closely related word icnoyo(t) in his 1571 dictionary and defined it as "compassionate" ("compasivo"), or "pious" ("piadoso").[7] In Huitzilan today the term generally refers to an ethic of behavior in which one takes into consideration the feelings and wishes of others rather than acts out of self-interest or impulse. Nacho explained that an icnot is a person who has respect, or icnoyot, as well as love, or tazohtaliz, and compassion, or teicneliliz, toward others. He declared on numerous occasions that respect (icnoyot), love (tazohtaliz), and compassion (teicneliliz) should exist in a marriage, in a family, and in a community.

Women frequently have the responsibility of teaching icnoyot to young children, and so I asked Antonia to explain what icnoyot meant to her, in a conversation that began when I remarked: "Many children today don't have respect." Antonia replied: "No. They act badly [ilapaquih]. Extremely so. Even though you hit them, they don't listen." In her response, the key word was ilapaquih, and when I asked Antonia what it meant, she replied: "fight" ("motehuia"). Her husband, Juan, added: "Fight with their siblings." The converse of the "ilapac," or disrespectful person, is the icnot, or the respectful one. Antonia's son, Eduardo, explained the meaning of the word icnoyot: "It means not acting inconsiderately. One just listens. If one does something bad to someone, he/she stops doing it." Nacho had explained that one who is a respectful person (icnot) has compassion, or teicneliliz. Antonia declared that to raise a child who is respectful and consequently has teicneliliz is an act of love, or tazohtaliz. She said: "Well, if you engender a child, you love him. And if you do not engender him, you don't love him." By engender, Antonia meant create, form, socialize, or educate.

Antonia and other Nahuat engender their children with a combination of love and punishment. Parents show love to their children in different ways. Antonia's husband, Juan, said that the kin term for "father" means love: "Tahueh means he who loves another." Eduardo, Antonia and Juan's son, declared that he tells his children that he loves them: "I'll say, 'I love you, papá.'" Antonia shows love to her children and grandchildren with caresses and hugs. However, the same woman who shows love to her children and grandchildren also can dish out harsh punishment for disrespectful behavior. When I asked Antonia how she taught icnoyot to her children and grandchildren, she mentioned discipline first: "Well, one hits them so that they'll calm down, so they won't do bad things, won't fight." She explained that she hits them with a switch, or "cuauhpitzac," but only three times, never to excess and never to hurt them. The number three refers to moderation because it is one short of four, the number representing a reasonable limit and the symbol Nahuat use for their quadrilateral view of the universe. Her son, Eduardo, explained that he also speaks to his children: "One talks to them. One says, 'Don't fight with your brother because you'll hurt him. And he'll hurt you too.'" The example of fighting with siblings as demonstrating a lack of respect came from Nahuat women and men who in 2003 had a vivid memory of the fratricidal conflict that erupted after the army chopped down the Talcuaco milpa.

Gabriela's Death

Nacho's mother, Gabriela, was unusually successful in inculcating respect in her family, measured by the length of time her sons remained working together to fill a common granary and purse. Gabriela died in 1978, and in Nacho's recollection of her death, as in his account of her life, he represented his mother as a person who took into consideration the hardships suffered by the other members of her family. He described her urging them not to spend their hard-earned money to find a cure for her illness, which Nacho described as old age. His narrative began when I asked him why she died.

Well, old age grabbed her. When it began, she said she always felt she wouldn't live. She said, "I'm ill now. Don't be curing me. You won't be curing me because I won't get better. I want to die now. Don't spend your money. You don't have it now. I'm going to die but you won't be curing me."

So then that's how it was. That's what she herself told us. And I, for being stubborn, I went to Teziutlan [a city on the edge of the northern sierra of Puebla], and I went to see one of those wise persons, those psychologists. Then the idea was that I go talk to her. I went for someone else. You knew Pascual Varela [a Nahuat]. He lost some money. And he said, "Go see a diviner about who took the money."

So I went. I went to see the diviner for that reason. I also asked that woman diviner for him. I said, "A man sent me who lost some money in Huitzilan. Tell me who took it."

"Oh, right there it's someone who visits him."

I asked, "What's the person's name?"

With a lot of effort she told me she was called Teresa. And there is no one named Teresa in Huitzilan. So then it wasn't true. That is, she couldn't really tell who stole the money. Then right away I said, "I've lost plenty. My mother is very, very ill. I want to know if she'll get well or won't get well."

"How old is she?" she asked.

"More or less seventy, seventy-five years old."

"Oh," she said. She started to stare at me, and she began to look at me and she said, "Your mother won't get better. She won't get well. Understand it. Don't suffer. Give her atole, perhaps tea. She'll ask for tea. Give it to her because nothing will work, it won't work anymore. It isn't going to work. She can't anymore, it's not possible for her to get better."

The Transition to Marriage

Nacho, like all Nahuat men, had to learn how to combine two kinds of love, or tazohtaliz, as he made the transition to marriage. On the one hand is love with respect, which he described when talking about nahueh. The other is love as desire, which a Nahuat man feels for his wife. Nacho revealed how he learned to combine the two meanings of love, or tazohtaliz, as he made the transition from living with his mother and brothers in Calyecapan to living with Victoria, first near her parents, and then in their own home in Talcez.

Chapters 8 and 9 present how Nacho made his transition over a period of time that began when he courted Victoria in 1970 and then settled down into a solid marriage with her. Nacho revealed how he made his transition when telling Orpheus myths about other men and women in 1970 and again in 1978, after he and Victoria had lived together for seven years. I shall interpret these myths as projections of his feelings about love with respect and love as desire at or around the time of their narration.

The projection of feelings into a story is one aspect of transference, which Nancy Chodorow defines as "the hypothesis and demonstration that our inner world of psychic reality helps to create, shape, and give meaning to the intersubjective social, and cultural worlds we inhabit." In projection, "we put feelings, beliefs, or parts of our self into an other."[8] The other, in this case, is both Victoria and the characters in the myths. Chapter 8 presents the Orpheus myth that Nacho told in 1970, representing the first stage in moving from his family in Calyecapan to his marriage with Victoria.

CHAPTER 8

Love as Desire

In 1970, when Nacho was courting Victoria, he told his first Orpheus myth, in which a man loved his wife more than she loved him. The wife was a woman who wasted time with men (cihuat ahuilnemi), a euphemism for a woman who has sex with a lot of different men. In this story, Nacho split his images of women into the bad wife and the good sister (icniuh) who tried to persuade her brother to leave his wayward wife. The brother, however, loved his bad wife with such a strong desire that he looked for her in the land of the dead.

This story is one of many that Nacho and other Nahuat narrators in Huitzilan told about men and women who acted on strong emotions and ended badly. As mentioned earlier, strong feelings come from the liver and can overwhelm more sublime emotions located in the animistic center of the heart. The woman in the first Orpheus tale ends up in the land of the dead with a demon lover who devours her in an act of cannibalistic sex. The husband, who follows her to the land of the dead, witnesses his wife in the primal scene with another man and returns to the land of the living without the object of his desire.

Nacho's 1970 Orpheus story expresses many concerns about a woman's loyalties that a man might feel when courting a woman he does not know well. The tale represents love as a desire, as a powerful, obsessive emotion that can drive a man to the land of the dead. His story was eerily prophetic because, like other narrators I knew during the earlier fieldwork (1968–1978), he anticipated how he would later attribute the arrival of the UCI in Huitzilan to a quarrel between Wolf and Dog over their obsessive desire to possess the same woman.

NACHO'S 1970 "ORPHEUS"

One day there was a woman who went about wasting a lot of time with men. And her husband never said anything to her because he really loved his wife. And that wife had sex with whomever she wanted. Her husband did not frighten her. And that man had a sister who told him, "Leave that woman. She wastes a lot of time, she wastes time with men."

That man did not pay her any heed. He wanted to be with his wife because she pleased him and he had pleasure with her. That woman had more sex with other men. She wasted all the time she wanted. And the day came when that woman went to do laundry with her sister-in-law. And her sister-in-law, the one who was the man's sister, she did not want to go.

"Let's go do the laundry," the wife said to her sister-in-law.

"I won't go," the sister-in-law replied. The man's sister was deciding what to do knowing that her sister-in-law spoke to many men. Many men detained her. "I won't go because I don't find what she does pleasant, and they'll grab her there in front of me."

"Let's go," the wife implored the sister.

The sister gave in and said yes, and the matter rested. And they were doing the laundry. A man appeared, that is to say a gentleman, and he said, "Now let's go to my house."

"No, I came here to do laundry."

"Yes? I'll give you money."

He gave her money and he grabbed her. He grabbed that woman; he put her on top of his horse and carried her off. Yes, that sister-in-law of hers returned home. The man arrived and he asked, "Where did the woman go?"

"Well I don't know," she said to him. "She went to wash, and a coyote seized her and took her. He gave her money and took her."

And that man started to feel sad. He started to weep.

"Not for her," she said to that boy. "It had to be I would take her and that woman would run off. No, you leave her. Now you see how she served you. She really wasted time with men."

"Yes, but I must go see her."

So he began his search and left to look for her. He went to look for her. And so he went and he went and reached what was perhaps a hilly place, whatever it was, and there were some men, those men were as black as beans.

"Where are you going?"

"Nowhere. I'm looking for a woman. Maybe you saw her? Maybe you saw where they took her?"

"Sure. We saw her, she passed through here. They took her."

"I want to go see her."

"Why did you come? No one comes, not here."

"I came because I'm looking for her."

"Well, how would you ever pass through now? You cannot pass through here. Well, this once we're going to go and drop you off, and you'll come right back. This one time we're going to drop you off."

"Good, I am going to see where my wife is."

They took him into a dangerous place. But who went where they took him through a big hollow mountain, that big dark place? It was completely dark. There wasn't anything. The wind was in his face. And they took him across.

"Your wife is here somewhere," said the being who perhaps was a man.

And afterwards so it was, they say, he went and found her and she was sewing.

"You've come!"

"Yes. I really looked for you."

"It's good that you've come. Don't be angry. Why have you come? No Earth Christian comes here."

"I've come because you left me when you came here."

"Ah yes, but don't be angry. I have another man here."

And he heard him come shouting.

"And just listen to him coming. Hide. Climb up into the loft."

He was inside a pot with a lid. He heard him shout closer.

"You're going to see him eat me and you'll see what he does to me."

And yes he saw that animal grab her. From there, that animal said to her, "I've come now."

"Yes, now you've come."

"I smell you're keeping an Earth Christian."

"No! Whom do you know who comes here? No one comes here. What you smell on me is from when I was on Earth and my husband fondled me."

Yes, that animal went to haul that woman towards him. From above, her husband saw him burrow into all of her bones. He ate all of her. Yes, he just left her heart. Yes, that man saw it all. He would be very frightened.

Afterwards that one who is not good left. Afterwards the husband was watching, and her heart started to slip and flip over backwards. It slipped and flipped over backwards, it slipped and flipped over backwards until she started to make herself whole, until she was as big as she was, until she made herself into a whole woman again. Yes. Now that man was also watching the same one who is not good.

"This is what you wanted," the demon said to her. "It would have been better if you hadn't seen your husband."

Yes, after the demon ate her, he finished and he left just her heart and he went away. From there, yes, then she started to make herself complete. She made herself whole, she made herself all whole and then she spoke to her husband.

"You saw clearly how he did me. Here, now take this money. Buy your clothes or eat with it. And this suit of your clothes, take it. I sewed it for you. Take it and put it on."

Yes, that man came back again. The one who dropped him off had waited for him, and he passed through to the outside. And he arrived. From there, yes. That man decided, "Well I shouldn't feel badly because I can't go again soon. I would like to. I'll feel badly. But I can't go, it isn't possible."

And that man climbed up out of the underworld and reached his sister.

"I've come back."

"You've come back. Did you find her?"

"Yes, I found her. I brought these clothes and this money. She told me to put the clothes on and she told me to buy something to eat with the money."

"Yes, but don't put the clothes on. Nor the money, don't eat with it."

That woman decided that the man should show them to a priest.

"This is what I did. I went to look for my wife until I found her. Here she always wasted time with men, and they took her from me. And I found her. She is down there. And she gave me these clothes and this money to buy something to eat."

"Ah yes," the priest said to him.

"Yes, and she has another one there, he who is not good."

"But these clothes, don't put them on because he'll eat you if you wear them. The same with the money. He put them here because he wanted you to find him. Don't put them on. If not, he won't take you. Now it would be better to burn the clothes and the money too. You're free. Look for another woman and you'll live better."

That man really believed him. He looked for another woman to marry. All of those clothes and money, the priest burned them for him.

"This is over. He wanted to eat you, but it won't be that way. Now we must burn these clothes and we must burn this money. And you should look for another woman and you will marry her and you will be better with her."

And there it ended.

Love as Desire

Nacho presented the husband's love as desire in several different ways. He used the verb tazohta, as in "he loved her" ("quitazohtaya"), but he made clear that he meant a different kind of love than what he felt when his mother was waiting for him with hot tortillas. Nacho indicated desire by describing the husband telling his sister that he does not want to leave his unfaithful wife because "she pleases him" ("cuallitta") and "he has pleasure with her" ("quipiya paquiliz ihuan yetoz"). To emphasize the intensity of the husband's desire, Nacho used the adverb "very much" ("cimi"), as in "he loved her very much" ("cimi quitazohtaya"), and he repeated the verb "to look for someone" ("temoa"), a common expression for love in Huitzilan, for emphasis.

He presented love as desire as a dangerous emotion by describing how the husband was so obsessed with his wife that he made the dangerous journey to the land of the dead and risked death itself. Nacho provided a detailed description of the land of the dead, telling how it is a dangerous place (ohuican), inside a big, hollow mountain (tepeconco), where it is very dark inside (yec tayohuayantihtoc) and one feels wind in the face (ehecatcaixco). A dangerous place suggests death, as does the mention of darkness. The sun's light and warmth are the source of the human soul (tonal), which enters through an infant's fontanel.[1] The mention of wind, particularly a cold wind, is common in Nahuat descriptions of the land of the dead, or "mictan." It was love as a powerful and dangerous desire that led to the death of many Nahuat, including Victoria, according to Nacho's story. I am referring, of course, to the dispute between Dog and Wolf that brought the UCI to Huitzilan.

The Unfaithful Woman

Nacho used the term "woman who wastes time with men," or "cihuat ahuilnemi," to describe the wife who was the object of the obsessive husband's desire. The term means a woman who has sex with many men rather than working with and for her husband. Nahuat in Huitzilan represent a marriage by saying a man and a woman "work for each other" (motequipanoah). Thus, a woman who wastes time with men (cihuat ahuilnemi) fails to do her share of the work because she is with other men and she does not love her husband. At the time Nacho told his first Orpheus tale, many stories of women who wasted their time with men circulated in the Nahuat oral tradition of the northern sierra of Puebla. More of them circulated in Huitzilan than in Yaonáhuac, where the Nahuat have lived comparatively free from mestizo pressure inside their community. The comparison of the same stories from the two communities revealed that Huitzilan narrators inserted more women who wasted time with men, or cihuat ahuilnemi, into their versions, apparently because they had more anxiety about the sexual loyalties of Nahuat women.[2]

Nacho made clear why he and other Nahuat men were apprehensive about a woman's sexual loyalty when he described how a mestizo carried the wife to the land of the dead. He represented the man as a mestizo in several unmistakable ways that included calling him a gentleman, or "caballero," describing him mounted on a horse, and referring to him as a coyote, or coyot. Nacho used the word "gentleman," or caballero, to refer to the man who carried off the wife, and his use of this word reflected the superior social position of the mestizos in Huitzilan at that particular time. His description of the caballero mounted on a horse is also an allusion to a mestizo. In my first two and a half years living in Huitzilan, between 1968 and 1970, I saw only mestizo men and occasionally women ride horses. At that time, horses, donkeys, and mules were the main forms of transportation from Huitzilan to Huahuaxtla, the closest community on a road passable by truck or car. The Nahuat always traveled by foot, sometimes carrying heavy loads with a huahcal and a tumpline. Nacho referred to the man as a "coyote," or coyot, a derogatory term for a mestizo I heard only in narratives and in conversation among the Nahuat. "Coyote" was a character in the popular trickster tale, which circulated in Huitzilan oral tradition between 1968 and 1978 and still enjoys enormous popularity today. As mentioned earlier, Coyote is greedy for meat, much as mestizos are greedy for land and Nahuat women. In 1970, many mestizo men married mestiza women and had children with Nahuat women. Rake was allegedly the father of sixty children in Huitzilan alone, and nearly all of the mothers of those children were Nahuat rather than mestiza women. It was difficult to determine why so many Nahuat women were willing to have children with Rake. Some probably needed his money, and a few reputedly became his lovers because he gave their fathers money. He might have taken others by force or by seduction, but only they know for certain. The tendency for men in a dominant group to eroticize women of the subordinate one is very common, as Ann Stoler and José Limón have noted.[3] Stories of the

exploits of Rake and other mestizo men circulated very widely in Huitzilan during my earlier fieldwork and probably fueled anxieties about the
loyalties of women like those expressed by Nacho in his first Orpheus
myth. There were many rumors that mestizos gave Nahuat men money
in exchange for sleeping with their daughters.

Nacho also alluded to other reasons closer to home that might make
a man feel sexual anxiety. He represented sex between the wife and her
demon lover as cannibalism, which could be a memory of witnessing the
primal scene in the cramped quarters of his house in Calyecapan. There
was little privacy for couples to have sex because couples did not sleep in
separate bedrooms. Nacho's brothers slept on separate mats from their
wives in a room with many other members of their extended families. If
one wanted to make love, he had to get up and move to the mat of his
wife and carry out lovemaking without benefit of a partition. Children
witnessed or heard the primal scene, which probably added to their impression of sexual desire as powerful and even unruly. Nacho ended his
1970 Orpheus myth by describing the husband witnessing his wife in
the primal scene with her demon lover and then returning to his sister.
Nacho's account of sex-as-cannibalism accords with memories of other
adults who witnessed the primal scene in their childhood.[4]

Splitting Images of Women

Nacho presented the sister as an ally who tried to warn her brother about
his wife who wasted time with men. In 2004, Nacho talked about the
sister in the 1970 Orpheus tale, saying: "She did a good thing for her
brother. She told him, 'That wife of yours. Be careful because she is
doing a bad thing'" ("Icneliaya icniuh. Quilia, 'Ne mocihuauh. Ticpiya
cuidado porque ne quichiuetoc mal'"). I have translated icneliaya, the
past tense of icneliā, as "she did a good thing" for her brother. Karttunen
defined icneliā as "to look after one's own welfare; to do a favor for
someone, to be charitable to someone."[5] It is the verb stem from which
the Nahuat form the noun teicneliliz, which Nacho and Karttunen both
define as "compassion, mercy, aid."[6] In the context of Nacho's exegesis
of his story, the word icneliā expresses the sister's love, or tazohtaliz, for
her brother. In 1970, Nacho had split his images of women into the good
sister and the bad wife, much as do many men struggling with Oedipal
anxieties compounded by predatory mestizo men, like Rake, who took
many women from Nahuat men.

Nacho's Courtship

In 2004, Nacho recalled a marked contrast between the marriage of the first Orpheus and his own developing relationship with Victoria during their courtship in 1970. In 2004, he interpreted the 1970 Orpheus as being in a marriage without reciprocal love and respect: "The man loved the woman. He lived crying for her because he loved her. That's why he looked for her. The woman did not love her husband. No, because anyone who has respect [icnoyot] in a couple, they love each other mutually. And they don't fool around."[7] By contrast, he recalled how, during his courtship with Victoria, they felt a mutual desire to be with each other as they fell in love. He said: "And since we went into the church a lot, we got a craving for each other [timonehnequeh]."[8] The term timonehnequeh, which I translated as "we got a craving for each other," is from the stem nehnequi, which Karttunen translated as "to pretend to be something one is not, to try to pass for someone else; to get a craving, to be capricious."[9] Nacho made clear that he meant that he and Victoria felt a strong attraction for each other because they had fallen in love.

Nacho undoubtedly idealized his courtship with Victoria when recounting his tragic love story in 2004. However, his 1978 Orpheus myth is one reason to conclude that he also changed his image of marital love at least eight years after his courtship, before Victoria's death. The seeds of that change appeared in other stories he told in 1970 in which he expressed his respect for women, perhaps because of his experiences with his own mother. Nacho showed that respect in the way he described the first meeting between Blancaflor and her lover Juan in the popular story of "Blancaflor" that circulated widely in Nahuat oral tradition prior to the UCI coming to Huitzilan. Nacho was unusual because he represented Blancaflor as acting with greater agency than did the other male narrators who told this same story. Usually, Juan comes upon Blancaflor bathing nude in the river. He snatches her clothes or jewelry and extracts a promise of help or marriage. A Nahua narrator from a different part of Mexico than Huitzilan described Juan carrying Blancaflor away by force. By contrast, Nacho toned down erotic imagery and gave Blancaflor more agency. His Blancaflor is not a nude bather but is washing clothes in the river. Juan does steal her jewelry, but his motive is to initiate a conversation, following the instructions of Mother Earth. Blancaflor has sufficient agency to set her own conditions for giving her promise of help; she demands that Juan take her away with him.[10] Blancaflor eventually becomes Juan's wife, and at the point they are about to marry, he addresses her as nahueh, the respectful and affectionate term for mother, perhaps because she will become the mother of their children.

These details are found only in Nacho's "Blancaflor" story, based on my comparison of variants I collected and that appear in published collections from Mexico and Spain. Nacho's representation of the first encounter between Juan and Blancaflor in 1970 shows how he respected women then and, thus, had the basis for moderating love as desire, or tazohtaliz, with respect, or icnoyot, and incorporating Victoria into his family. I believe that the Orpheus myth he told in 1978, after he and Victoria had lived together as man and wife for seven years, revealed that he had done so long before her death in 1983. It is to that 1978 Orpheus that I now turn.

CHAPTER 9

Wife as Sister

In 1978, Nacho told his second Orpheus myth in front of Victoria and his children, Epifania and Alfonso. This time he turned the wife into a sister. As noted in Chapter 8, the sister in the earlier Orpheus tale did a good turn for her brother by persuading him to leave his unfaithful wife and find another woman. Nacho's transformation of the wife into a sister appears to be one way he combined love-as-desire with respect, and it appears to express how his courtship had led to a solid marriage.[1] In essence, Victoria had become a nahueh, the term Nacho used for his young nieces, for his mother, and, in his version of "Blancaflor," for a wife.

Nacho identified the wife as a sister and made her marriage to her brother clear by saying that "they served each other," or "motequipano-huayah," based on the verb "to work, to serve someone" (tequipanoa).[2] The Nahuat of Huitzilan frequently referred to a marriage with this verb.[3] However, the sister is a prohibited object of a man's carnal affections according to Nahuat morality. A man or a woman may not marry or have sex with a blood relative, and the Nahuat frequently express the prohibition as forbidding anyone from marrying an icniuh. The Nahuat of Huitzilan apply the term sibling, icniuh, to a brother or a sister and to any blood relative in the speaker's generation. Thus the brother and sister who lived together as man and wife in Nacho's Orpheus myth have broken a serious prohibition. As a consequence, the sister-wife must endure being in the land of the dead with a cannibalistic demon lover because she broke the rule of sibling incest.

Nevertheless, Nacho cast the sister very differently than he did the wife "who wasted time with men" in the earlier Orpheus myth he told while courting Victoria. In the first Orpheus tale, the wife betrayed her husband with many men, including a wealthy mestizo. In this second myth, the sister is not unfaithful to her brother while she remains in the land of the living. In the earlier version, the priest persuaded the husband not to wear the clothes and eat with the money his wayward wife had given him in the land of the dead. In this Orpheus myth, the priest helps the brother see his sister in the land of the dead. And the sister's demon lover is a goat, an animal linked to the devil for sure, but only indirectly associated with the Spanish-speakers whose ancestors had brought goats to Mexico from the Old World.

NACHO'S 1978 "ORPHEUS"

One day there were two siblings. One was a man and one was a woman. And they loved one another, the woman as much as the man. The woman never had a man, and the boy also did not have a woman. They loved each other. They just served each other. And the day came when the sister died. She died. And from there, yes, he lived looking for her. He looked for his sister. She died. And he really looked for her. He didn't know where she was. He lived crying for her. So then he went to see the priest.

"I really look for my sister. Where can I find her?"

"Do you want to see her?"

"Yes, I want to see her."

Then the priest opened the place where the dead pass by in a procession. The priest went to open that place, and the brother went to see her.

"You'll find her sewing," said the priest.

That man went. He went to see his sister. They say she was sewing a blanket.

"You've come!" she said to him.

"Yes, I've come. I really looked for you until I didn't know what. I really look for you until I don't know how I shall be."

"You should not have come. You came here because you had to. No one else comes here."

"But I came. I really looked for you until I don't know what."

"But you shouldn't have come. I have a man here. I have a man here who rules me. Now you're going to see him because he'll come. Don't you hear the man shouting? He comes shouting from far away. And listen to him come now. He'll see you because he's coming right away. Climb up into the loft."

He climbed up into the loft and went into a big pot.

"And go in here, and I'm going to cover you with the lid. You keep that

*lid on over you. Peek at me from up there and with just one of your eyes.
You'll be able to look down at how the man comes."*

*The brother heard him come closer. The woman's man arrived now. The
brother heard him come shouting again.*

"And here he comes now," says the sister.

*Her man arrived standing in the corridor. The brother saw that the
man's mouth was down to here [Nacho gestures to the waist]. He was a
goat. He was really sniffing in the corridor as he came to see her.*

"I smell that you're keeping meat here," he said to her.

"No," replied the sister.

*"No, I smell an Earth Christian you're keeping here. You're keeping him
here."*

"No, how could he be here?"

"He sure is here."

*"My clothes still have the scent of the crotch from where I came. But no
one is here."*

"Yes, you're keeping him."

*"No, I'm not keeping him. I'm not keeping him. How can you say I am?
There isn't anyone here."*

*Then, they say, that animal came over and grabbed her and scared his
wife. He frightened her and started to eat her. He finished eating her; he
left just a little of her. He left just her heart. From there yes. He made a
loud cracking noise as he finished eating everything. He just left her heart.
Then that animal went away. The brother saw everything the animal did.
What he saw frightened him. He was scared. He watched her heart. It
slipped and flipped over backwards on the ground. It slipped and flipped
over backwards. It slipped and flipped over backwards. She started to revive
herself; her heart re-formed her. She began to slip and flip over backwards
until she made herself whole, the woman made herself whole until she
reappeared.*

"Come down," she said to her brother.

He came down.

*"You saw clearly what happened to me. He's the man I'm with. Now
you saw what happened to me. It'd be better for you to work and look for a
woman. Look for a woman so you don't do to yourself what I did to myself.
Look for a woman and work. And take some money I've been gleaning from
him. Wait for me. I'll go where you are. I'll go there tomorrow, and watch
for me to appear down by your foot. Wait for me."*

*They say the man came back. He came back and he was waiting and
watching for his sister's soul to appear. He saw a fly appear. It was one of*

those big flies. He saw it appear. It started walking. He hit it with his hat.
Then that next day he went again.
　"You didn't tell me the truth."
　"I went, and you just hit me."
　"That was really you? How could it be?"
　"I went there. I went there."
　That's how he realized a flying insect was a soul. There are many of
them. There are many of those flying insects. They say souls are flying in-
sects, that is, they're flies.

There are a number reasons why Nacho cast the wife as a sister in his
1978 Orpheus myth when he knew that there was a strong prohibition
on sibling incest in his culture. One could be the clash between taboo
and desire observed by Malinowski among the Trobriands, who told a
myth of forbidden love between a brother and sister, while having a very
strong sibling incest taboo.[4] Malinowski believed that the strength of the
taboo brought about an "irresistible fascination with forbidden fruit."[5]
Melford Spiro argued that Trobriand men recast their childhood Oedipal wish as a desire for the sister, who "more than anyone else most re-
sembles the mother of childhood."[6] Some support for Spiro's psychoanalytic interpretation comes from ethnographic reports from around the
world, where brother-and-sister incest is a common theme in creation
mythology.[7]

In Nahua antiquity, the sister was also an erotic object in a number
of texts. The ancient priest-king Topiltzin-Quetzalcoatl called for his sister when drunk on pulque, according to the sixteenth-century *Annals of
Cuauhtitlan*.[8] Nahua hunters used erotic imagery when addressing deer
as older sister, according to the seventeenth-century *Treatise on Superstitions,* by Hernando Ruiz de Alarcón.[9] Contemporary Nahuat continue to
represent the brother and sister as charged with suppressed erotic desire,
although usually in a negative way. Narrators in Huitzilan told stories of
brothers and sisters who loved each other but had to separate once the
sister experienced her sexual awakening with another man (a mestizo).[10]
The stories dramatize the necessity of the actual separation of many
brothers and sisters by sending the sister to live in patrilocal residence
with her husband shortly after she has her first menstrual period.[11]

Victoria had probably become like a sister to Nacho as they raised
their children and lived and worked together in their Talcez home. The
1978 story appears to present the kind of love that a man might feel for a
woman who is nahueh and the focus of his erotic interest. As mentioned

earlier, Nacho and other Nahuat men use the term nahueh to refer to mother, to a girl who might be a sister, or icniuh, and who may become a mother, and to a woman who is or will become a wife. After several years of marriage, Nacho and Victoria probably felt as trustful and familiar as if they were siblings. The concept of respect, or icnoyot, which Nacho and many other Nahuat say should prevail in a marriage, requires that a man observe a six-month postpartum sexual taboo, as Nacho explained to me in his Talcez home, in front of Victoria. In this sense, the meaning of icnoyot includes sexual restraint or modesty such as one finds in any well-managed Nahuat family.[12]

Nacho and Victoria, 1973–1978

Between 1973 and 1978, I visited Nacho and Victoria in their Talcez home on a daily basis whenever I was in Huitzilan. I once asked Victoria about rumors of wife-beating in other couples that circulated every now and again, and she said firmly: "I would not take that from any man." She also affirmed on more than one occasion that Nacho was a good husband to her. During my daily visits, Nacho and Victoria were usually both at home. Nacho spent a great deal of time selling thread to young girls and women, who were embroidering the collars and sleeves of women's blouses.[13] He talked a lot about colors because his customers were in the middle of embroidery projects and wanted to match exactly the thread they had been using before buying more. Both Victoria and Nacho watched over their two children, Epifania and Alfonso, and Victoria cooked and washed. Nacho occasionally went to his cornfield, or milpa, and also brought in a little extra money by selling coffee growing on a small plot of land he had inherited from his father.

Once, in the presence of Nacho, Victoria told me voluntarily that she had taken contraceptive injections because she had given birth to three children, and the resident doctor advised her to wait for a while before having more children. Victoria seemed relieved because she was constantly washing Epifania and Alfonso's diapers and seemed particularly burdened with toil and responsibility. Her first child had died in infancy while she and Nacho were living with her father at the southern end of the community. Someone murdered the doctor—apparently he had the reputation as a womanizer—and Victoria gave birth to three more children after I left Huitzilan in 1978. Between 1973 and 1978, Victoria and Nacho seemed to have a relationship of relative equality. He did not seem to dominate her, and she did not seem to dominate him in any way that was visible to someone who spent a great deal of time in their presence. Victoria was always warm and gracious, and she and Nacho seemed to have a good sense of humor with each other.

Recalling His Marriage in 2004

In 2004, Nacho represented his marriage with Victoria the same way he described the brother and sister loving each other mutually and deeply in the Orpheus myth he told in 1978. In the myth he described mutual love between the brother and the sister by saying: "They loved each other, the woman as much as the man."[14] In 2004, he also described, in a typical Nahuat way, mutual love with respect in his marriage: "We loved each other. Just as I loved her, she loved me a lot, and I never hit her, nor did she hit me. We loved each other beautifully. We quarreled. I scolded her. She scolded me. But that's where it ended. We did not hit each other."[15] The symmetry in this statement is characteristic of relationships of respect, or icnoyot. He remembered Victoria as treating and loving him the way he treated and loved her. His use of the expression "we did not hit each other," or "ahmo timotehuiayah," is very common among Nahuat couples in Huitzilan to describe a marriage in which there is respect. The key word in this expression is "timotehuiayah," which is the first person plural past tense of tehuia, which means "to get struck with stones; to strike, pound something with stones."[16] Usually the verb refers to couples doing physical harm to each other with hands or fists, as well as with stones. The Nahuat use this verb to refer to a level of quarreling that, if exceeded, means a marriage without respect.

Also in his tragic love story of 2004, he described his grief upon hearing the news of Victoria's death in ways similar to how he presented the brother grieving for his sister in 1978. In the myth he said: "The brother loved his sister deeply, and because of his deep love, he suffered greatly when his sister died." Nacho added: "he lived looking for her" ("quitemotinemi"); "he really looked for her" ("melauh quitemoa"); and "he lived crying for her" ("chocatinemi"). The brother became so disoriented by his grief that he no longer knew where he was. Nacho changed verb tenses to indicate the brother's temporal as well as spatial disorientation. The brother said: "I really look for you until I don't know how I shall be" ("Melauh nimitztemoa hasta ahmo nicmati quenieu niyetoz"). I checked with Nacho about his verbs, and he said they were correct and that he intended to mean temporal as well as spatial disorientation in representing the depth of the brother's grief.

In 2004, he employed some of the same spatial imagery when describing the depth of his shock and grief upon hearing the news from Sebastiana Arellano that Victoria had died in a massacre. He recalled that he said to his patrón what I translated as: "They took my wife from me." He actually said, "Nechquitehuiqueh nocihuauh," which could mean different things depending on how one interprets the verb tehuiqueh. He could mean tehuiqueh, as in "they struck her with stones [or bullets]," or tehuīqueh, as in "they took her away from me." Much depends on where one places the stress. I carefully went over this passage with Nacho, and he said he intended both meanings. The phrase "they took my wife from me" is the complementary opposite of the verb temoa, meaning "to look for someone," which expresses finding or hoping to find one's love. Nacho also described in his narrative of actual grief that he was so distressed he became disoriented in space. He said: "Fiero hasta ma campa nimopolihui nicmachiliaya," meaning "I felt so bad that I felt lost where I was." Nacho's use of spatial imagery to express feelings of love and loss, imagery that he used in the narratives he told in 1970, 1978, and 2004, is an example of how personal memory can converge with collective memory or culture. It would be wrong to conclude, however, that Nacho's personal memory reduces to collective memory. As Ricoeur explained, the two are "distinct, yet reciprocal and interconnected."[17] I interpret the coincidence between the imagery he used in 1978 and again in 2004 as an example of how he found in his culture the language to express his feelings of shock and loss when he recalled how he felt when he heard the news of Victoria's death.

Nacho's description of the love between a brother and sister in his 1978 Orpheus also accords with how he remembered his feelings for Victoria in 2004. At that time he said: "I feel I loved her because I felt it inside, in my heart, that I would never find another woman like her. There isn't another woman who loved me like she did. And just as she loved me a lot, I didn't want anything to hurt her. I didn't want her to be hungry. I didn't want her to eat anything bad, not even a little fly. I loved her with all my heart."[18] Nacho kept a vivid memory of how Victoria worried about him, which is one way that he knew she loved him. "I knew that she loved me because she wouldn't eat if I didn't eat with her. If I went to Zacapoaxtla, and arrived home late, she waited for me. She didn't eat. Only if I ate then she'd eat with me. If I didn't come home, she was crying. She was looking for me. If I went to the milpa, she let me know that she was crying because I didn't come home. That's how I knew she loved me."[19]

Other experiences Nacho had between 1978 and Victoria's death in 1983 may have contributed to this memory of his feelings for Victoria of which he spoke many years later. During the interval between telling the second story of Orpheus and the massacre in which Victoria died, she and Nacho probably became closer as they faced the threats from the UCI together. Nacho had recalled how Victoria had saved him from Wrath, who had come to kill him in the church. Nacho had remembered her confronting Wrath face-to-face and telling him: "Let go of my husband because he isn't doing anything to you." The tone of Nacho's voice as he repeated Victoria's words in Nahuat—"Xicahua noyoquich porque ahmo teyi mitzchihuilitoc"—as she had probably pronounced them in the voice of an angry woman (tahuel cihuat), made me think that Nacho was reliving this moment at the base of the church tower. This remembrance seems to be what Ricoeur means by "memory as passion," as distinct from recollection, which involves the act of searching.[20]

Mourning and Melancholia

The way one grieves is related to how one loves, according to Freud in his classic paper "Mourning and Melancholia."[21] Mourning refers to the pain and loss one feels for the death of a loved one. Melancholia is "a lowering of the self-regarding feelings to a degree that finds utterance in self-reproaches and self-reviling, and culminates in a delusional expectation of punishment."[22] In the case he presented, a woman who displayed the symptoms of melancholia had fallen out of love with her dead husband and felt guilty about it.

However, the expressions of love and grief also vary with cultural and historical experience, as Nancy Scheper-Hughes discovered in her study of women in northwest Brazil. The Brazilian women had endured years of neglect and betrayal and were "coached in the art of resignation" so that their emotions would not "run riot" and make them sick.[23] Scheper-Hughes notes that Brazilians celebrate maternal love in their folklore, folk art, popular culture, and devotion to saints. However, any maternal optimism that a woman might feel soon after the birth of her child gives way to "pessimism, doubt, and despair rooted in the unhappy experience of repeated infant death."[24]

Perhaps infant deaths and hardship are two of the reasons that the

Nahuat told so many stories showing why strong feelings, or ilihuizti, always lead to a bad result. However, the Nahuat try to cultivate sublime forms of love through language and ritual, as Nacho explained at many points in this book. It remains to be seen if and how Nahuat women express love and grief differently than Nahuat men. There are a number of similarities in Epifania's and Nacho's expressions of love and grief for Victoria, but I suspect that more research will also uncover important differences. In other cultures, men and women sometimes use language differently when expressing love and grief, as Lila Abu-Lughod discovered among Bedouin men and women she studied in Egypt.[25]

There are indications that Mesoamerican women do grieve differently than men, judging from studies by anthropologists working in other parts of Mexico and in Guatemala. Anne Woodrick reported that a Yucatec Mayan woman could only love without ambivalence someone who had died. The woman explained it was the evil flesh that prevented her from loving a living person.[26] Judith Zur reported that some K'iche' war widows felt "dirty since *la violencia;* they are concerned to present themselves well but . . . show a preoccupation with being literally dirty."[27] Zur worked with five widows, only one of whom appeared to have had an affectionate relationship with her husband.[28] The other four appear to have experienced melancholia when remembering their husbands, who, when drunk, had beaten them, sometimes severely. When recollecting their sons, however, they displayed mourning like that which Nacho remembered feeling for Victoria.

CHAPTER 10

Conclusions

Ruth Behar remarked that death "leaves us on the brink between silence and speech."[1] Nacho chose speech, and his choice of words and the tone he conveyed when pronouncing those words made me think I could feel what he felt. He spoke from his memory, many years after the events he described had taken place. He seemed to relive when he courted Victoria in the church, when Victoria saved him from Wrath at the base of the bell tower, when Wrath and Dog's son came to kill him a second time in the church, when he heard the news of Victoria's death, when he struggled to take care of his young children, and when he learned of Manuela's death several years later. He closed his three-day narrative with the words "I always remember." ("Siempre niquelnamiqui.")

When it comes to remembering feelings, Ricoeur reminds us that "memory is, in fact, capable of recalling joy without being joyful, and sadness without being sad."[2] It depends on whether remembering is memory as passion or recollection.[3] Memory as passion is when one feels today as if it were yesterday, whereas recollection is the act of scouring one's memory to reconstruct the past. Memory as passion is a complicated concept because, as Ricoeur again reminds us, Aristotle asked: "What is it that we remember? Is it the affection or the thing that produced it? If it is affection, then it is not something absent one remembers; if it is the thing, then how, while perceiving the impression, could we remember the absent thing that we are not at present perceiving? In other words, while perceiving an image, how can we remember something distinct from it?"[4] The solution to this question is to distinguish between external stimulation and internal resemblance.[5] These two aspects of memory—external stimulation and internal resemblance—operate in what psychoanalytic theorists call transference. Nancy Chodorow defined transference as drawing from our inner world "to create, shape, and give meaning" to the world we inhabit.[6] What did Nacho use from his inner world to give meaning to the world he inhabits in the narrative he told when remembering Victoria, and what does it matter in "the life-line of the world," to borrow from Geertz?[7]

I believe the answer to both questions is what he said about tazohta-liz in all of the meanings he gave that word in his narratives. When re-membering how Victoria loved him, he said she would not eat until he arrived safely home and could eat with her. He remembered she told him she cried if he came home late from his milpa and she looked for him in her imagination as she wondered where he was. And, of course, Nacho remembered that Victoria saved him from Wrath, who was about to kill him at the base of the bell tower a few months before she died. He also recalled how he learned from his mother the meaning of tazohtaliz, and told how she was waiting for him with his tortillas and wanted him to come back soon to pay her a visit. He added she came to visit him and brought him meals when he was living with Victoria first in Miyacaco and then in Talcez.

A number of things stand out in these memories, and one is that they involve his feelings of Eros, or attachment to women. Bowlby and his team of observers made careful observations of mothers and infants and concluded that feelings of attachment and loss are precultural and quite possibly universal emotions.[8] We know, of course, that maternal attach-ment may not develop under conditions of extreme deprivation, as Nancy Scheper-Hughes discovered in her study of grief in Brazil.[9]

Freud believed Eros is what usually holds us together, and he distin-guished this feeling from Thanatos, which he attributed to his maligned concept of the death instinct. Writing at the time the Nazis were coming to power in Germany, he declared that a society must spend more energy controlling Thanatos than managing Eros.[10] Nacho might agree with him because he attributed Victoria's death to the anger, or cualayot, that erupted after the army chopped down the UCI's milpa. However, he also considered sexual desire, the root of Eros according to Freud, as a troublesome and unruly emotion that caused Dog to join Wrath in invit-ing Felipe Reyes to Huitzilan.

Nacho's memories of tazohtaliz raise questions about the relationship between personal and collective memory. For example, he associated food with women's love: he remembered his mother inviting him to eat and offering him food; he recalled Victoria, in the manner of a sister, waiting to share her food with him. Anthropologists such as Carole Counihan have noted the association between food and love on the grounds that both are happy or pleasant memories felt in the body.[11]

Nacho's memory of food and women's love is also related to the role that Nahuat women play in creating human goodness, or love and respect, by offering food to their male partners during the flower tree, or xochicuahuit, rituals. These rituals have a shared meaning, or are part of Nahuat culture or collective memory.[12] Other shared memories of love also appeared in his 2004 narrative, and they include representing love in spatial terms. "To look for another" ("temoa") or move toward another in space is a common expression of love and was the main theme of the Orpheus stories Nacho told in 1970 and 1978.

Nacho's use of images found in other narratives to express feelings for Victoria in 2004 is not the whole story of his memory. I think he actually felt Victoria's love for him and his love for her in 2004, after she had been dead for twenty-one years. To be sure, he may have idealized her after she had gone to the land of the dead, but his Orpheus tale of 1978 also revealed that, at the time of narration, he felt he shared a strong mutual love with her much like the brother and sister in the story. If true, then his memory included actual feelings he had for Victoria five years before her death, which may have become even stronger as they faced together the threat of the UCI.

Does it matter that one Nahuat man spoke so eloquently about his love for his dead wife? I think it does because his words help to round out our picture of indigenous speakers in Mexico and Guatemala. There are many life histories from this part of the world, but very few contain much information on feelings of attachment, which are supposed to be precultural or universal in the human condition. We have descriptions of fear, anger, envy, and sexual desire but none, to my knowledge, for the meanings of indigenous words such as tazohtaliz, particularly in marriage. There are very few autobiographical love stories in any Amerindian language, despite the Orpheus stories in Native American oral tradition. If oral narratives are collective memories, then how can there be collective, but no personal, memories of love and loss in the same society? Do love stories only exist in the imagination but not in the lives of real people? I think not. To neglect to recognize the full range of emotional expression in the narratives of a people is to infantilize them, or reduce them to Freud's neurotic primitive.[13]

Anthropologists have observed love in many other parts of the non-Western world: Evans-Pritchard described "romantic love" in Nuer courtship;[14] and Meyer Fortes found evidence of deep and enduring love among some Tallensi couples in Africa.[15] Romantic love in its European form may indeed be a relatively recent European invention, although some believe it is more widespread than originally thought.[16] Nacho's idea of tazohtaliz is different from romantic love as I observed it in Spain. Spanish men said in their stories that they idealized women for their beauty, and women said in their versions of the same stories that they were skeptical of men who fell in love with them on first sight because they were beautiful.[17] Nacho, when recalling his courtship, did not say he and Victoria idealized each other. Rather, he said: "we got a craving for each other." To have a craving is to have desire, an unruly part of tazohtaliz that can become an obsession one should avoid. Thus he had to transform his desire into a love like that which a brother has for a sister.

Nacho and Victoria developed a brother-and-sisterly love by working together, or motequipanoah. As Catherine Good observed for another group of Nahuas, working together creates love between people.[18] Nacho explained the relationship between love and work in the following way: "When someone works, one sees that he or she is a good person. If you work together well with another, one loves that person because he or she is doing what I would do but cannot do alone."[19] When applying this idea to a marriage, he said: "We think that if there is a man but no woman, it does not make a whole. And it is the same for the woman. If she does not have a man, it does not make a whole."[20] He dramatized this point by describing how he suffered after Victoria's death as he did the work of two people to take care of their five small children.

The form of tazohtaliz he developed with Victoria was different from the love a man has for a woman that Freud had in mind when he described the predicament of the Western man. According to Freud, man idealizes woman as a sexual object, while woman is forced into the position of being admired for her beauty.[21] Man loves woman who loves her child, and neither man nor woman can have the object of desire. Rather, both are doomed to be discontented because woman becomes estranged from man and the child becomes estranged from woman.[22] Jane Gallop summarized this predicament with her cryptic observation that man and woman are "a phase apart."[23] Many Western novels describe this predicament. One is Hemingway's *A Farewell to Arms*, which, among other things, tells of a man who fell in love with a woman only to fall into deep despair when the woman dies in childbirth.

Nacho was in a different predicament because his notion of tazohtaliz was not the same as the Western notion of romantic love. One cannot rule out that Spaniards introduced a concept of love that became part of the contemporary meanings of tazohtaliz. Louise Burkhart described how the friars sponsored the translation of Spanish plays, such as *Holy Wednesday,* representing Mary's deep love and anticipated grief for Christ as he was headed for his Crucifixion. However, Burkhart also demonstrated how the Nahuatl subtly changed the meaning of many aspects of this play in the act of translation.[24]

Nacho's idea of tazohtaliz seems to have the meaning of love that Quezada had in mind when hypothesizing about the ancient Nahuas.[25] Nacho, like others in his community, described, in his stories, women with the power to produce vast quantities of food from a single kernel of corn or a single bean. Behind his appreciation for the procreative power of women was the way he valued children, and when remembering Victoria in 2004, he recalled how he immediately asked Sebastiana Arellano about his children upon hearing the terrible news of Victoria's death. Again, when he heard of Manuela's death, he recalled hearing the person on the phone remind him that he still had his children. And, of course, he still lives with two of his children in an extended family household in Talcez. Nacho, unlike the Western European man of Freud and Hemingway, directed his tazohtaliz to his children as well as to the woman with whom he shared a great love. I do not know if that made his grief any less than that of Hemingway's protagonist, but I do think it made his grief different. Although Nacho may have felt different than Freud's discontented man and Hemingway's heartbroken hero, I hope his story of love and grief has conveyed his humanity.

Hemingway's *A Farewell to Arms* is more than a love story; for Alvin Rosenfeld it also tells of the "collapse of a whole idealized code that once sustained life by giving it a measure of purpose and honor."[26] One could say something similar about Nacho's tragic love story. His tale describes how the conflict over Talcuaco changed Huitzilan in very profound ways, perhaps marking the end of the Nahuat hope to restore or maintain a culture based on the communal production of corn. It challenged faith in a moral system built on love (tazohtaliz), human goodness (cualtacayot), and respect (icnoyot) by which one is supposed to control destructive emotions such as anger (cualayot), fear (mauhcayot), and desire (another form of tazohtaliz). Nacho's personal history is filled with grief for Victoria and for all of the Nahuat who suffered when those in the UCI turned against their brothers following the destruction of the Talcuaco cornfield. It also contains a ray of hope, however tenuous, when telling how the flower-tree rituals can restore human goodness and when revealing how Nacho has carried on by working and living with his children in love and respect.

Notes

Chapter 1

1. Taggart 1975, 97–103, 106–108.
2. Quiñones Keber 1995, 29, 183.
3. According to Frances Karttunen (1983, 104), the Nahuatl verb (i)lnāmiquil(i) means "for memory to return, sharpen; to remember, reflect on something." In the sierra Nahuat dialect of Nahuatl, the verb is quelnāmiqui, which means "to remember something or someone," and the noun for memory is tēlnāmiquiliz.
4. Ricoeur 2006 (2004), 8.
5. See Weisman (2004, 55) on Primo Levi's assessment of Holocaust survivor testimonies. Michael Kenny (1999) raised similar questions about the use of testimonies in anthropology.
6. Robert Laughlin (1962) was one of the first to call attention to this tradition in indigenous-speaking Mexico.
7. Anthropologists have noted the parallels and the differences between Western literary concepts and those in other cultures. See Elizabeth Colson's (1971) very sensitive account of the meanings of courage and heroism in Tonga culture.
8. There are comparatively few autobiographical accounts of love among Native Americans on either side of the border between Mexico and the United States. Native Americans do talk of love in the stories of their Orpheus tradition (Gayton 1935). Scholars, however, have interpreted the Orpheus tales in this tradition in other ways. See Hultkrantz (1957) and Swanson (1976).
9. Independent information to place memories in a historical perspective is useful for many reasons. Memory changes over time, individual memory converges with collective memory, and cultural notions of time and space affect the recollection of chronological events (Vansina 1985, 160–173). Testimonies of the past often bear the stamp of subsequent experiences (Vansina 1985, 161; Kenny 1999; Weisman 2004). Vincent Crapanzano (1985 [1980]) cautioned against psychological reconstructions, noting that they fail to take into consideration the relationship between the subject and the life history researcher.

10. The historical and ethnographic record is replete with accounts of the pain, sadness, fear, and anger of those who lived through colonialism and its aftermath (Harkin 2003). One account that is relevant for the Nahuat case is Miguel León Portilla's (1970 [1964]) moving compilation of the testimonies of the ancient Nahuas' reaction to the Spanish Conquest of Mexico. I have taken a life history approach (Langness and Frank 1981) in this work, which is based on the autobiographical statements of Nacho and others in his community. Paul Radin (1926) was one of the first to use this approach with his Winnebago subject, Crashing Thunder, who wrote of his pain, despair, and anger as he experienced the disintegration of his culture. Nancy Lurie (1966 [1961]) provided a vivid picture of the feelings of Crashing Thunder's sister, Mountain Wolf Woman.

11. Nacho revealed many meanings of the word tazohtaliz by using it in different contexts. See Sherzer (1983) and Briggs (1988) for linguistic studies on the relationship between meaning and context.

12. Molina 1966, 16. The main difference between Nahuatl and Nahuat is that Nahuat "lost the characteristic lateral release of TL" (Karttunen 1983, xxi). I added the parenthetical "h" to Molina's spelling of tlazo(h)tlaliz to represent a missing glottal stop.

13. Molina 1966, 16.

14. I shall use the term "Nahua" to refer to the many different dialects of related languages spoken in Central Mexico. The two main dialects are Nahuatl, spoken in the Valley of Mexico, Tlaxcala, Puebla, Veracruz, Hidalgo, Durango, and Guerrero, and Nahuat, spoken in the northern sierra of Puebla.

15. López Austin 1988 (1980), 181, 190, 192.

16. See Taggart 1997. López Austin (1988 [1980], 191) translates ilihuiz as "imprudent."

17. López Austin (1988 [1980], 193–194) noted that the heart is the most important center of vital forces for contemporary as well as ancient speakers of indigenous languages. He noted that Guiteras Holmes (1965, 246–247) identified the heart as a center for the emotions of a Tzotzil (Mayan) subject.

18. "Ticehuah toyollo."

19. "Nehha nicmachilia nictazohta porque nicmachia tech noihtic, tech noyollo."

20. "Tel huei tayolcol."

21. James 1997, 121.

22. Taggart 1990.

23. Pitt-Rivers 1966, 94. See Taggart (1990, 93–115) for men's and women's representations of romantic love in Spanish folktales.

24. Quezada 1975, 26–27; 1996.

25. Quiñones Keber 1995, 29, 183. See also Graulich 1997, 57.

26. Taggart 1997 (1983), 114–160.

27. Gossen 1994, 556.

28. Nash 1997.

29. Many of the pressures on the Nahuat are a result of globalization, which June Nash (2001, 1) defined as a process driven by "the penetration of unregulated market exchanges" that causes in communalistic societies the "'fragmentation' or atomization of personal relations and political units, the 'homogeniza-

tion' or 'hybridization' of culture, and the 'alienation' of people from community, kin groups, and even self."

30. Taggart 1997 (1983).

31. See Taussig (1980). Evidence that the position of indigenous women declined, adversely affecting marriage, comes from several sources. Susan Kellogg (1995) found that the Spanish courts treated Nahuatl women juridically as minors. Bernard Levallé (1999, 21–22, 27, 32) found ample evidence in annulment and divorce records of "indigenous" men mistreating their wives in colonial Peru. Oscar Lewis (1949) described role conflict between Nahuatl husbands and wives in Mexico. Lewis (1967 [1964]) also reported that his Nahuatl subject, Pedro Martínez, was at times cruel and unfaithful to his wife, Esperanza. Chevalier and Buckles (1995, 243) describe the "many problems that poverty-stricken men and women face when uprooted from their kin-based mode of livelihood and subjected to a broader market economy over which they have no control." In formerly Nahua-speaking communities in some parts of Mexico, men split their images of women between the asexual and revered mother and the unworthy whore, adversely affecting marriage (Friedlander 1975; Ingham 1986). Rovira (2002) contrasts the unhappy marriage of "traditional" villagers with the happy ones of those who joined progressive movements such as the Zapatistas. Underlying some of this work is the idea that men who are speakers of indigenous languages have a hatred of women. See Earle and Simonelli (2005, 101) for a description of what they call Mayan feminists who run counter to this trend.

32. Schryer (1990, 47–48) reported that the Nahuatl in the Huasteca of Hidalgo invaded a pasture belonging to one of the richest Nahuatl in Pepeyocatitla in 1971.

33. Camahji 1979, 2.

34. Ejército Zapatista de Liberación Nacional, or Zapatista Army of National Liberation. See Collier and Quaratiello (1999 [1994]) for a description of the historical conditions giving rise to the Zapatista movement in Chiapas.

35. Schryer 1990, 11. Schryer (1990, 11) declared that by using his method it was "impossible to obtain the amount of detailed information or the type of inside picture of daily life so characteristic of anthropological research in a single village or municipio."

36. See Higgins (2004) on the invisibility of indigenous speakers in Mexico. Ironically, Judith Friedlander (1975) argued that the Nahuatl-speakers of Hueyapan, Morelos, had a lower-class rather than indigenous culture at the same time that the Nahuas of the northern sierra of Puebla and the Huasteca of Hidalgo were carrying out land invasions (see Schryer 1990). The land invasions had nativistic elements, as do the rituals of blood sacrifice indigenous-speakers have carried out in the Huasteca of Veracruz (Sandstrom in press).

37. Zur (1998) and Green (1999). See Scheper-Hughes (1996), who urged anthropologists to study small wars.

38. Green 1999, 12, 14. Watanabe (1992) and Stoll (1993) describe Mayan communities that managed to escape or at least contain the level of internal violence during the Guatemalan civil war. Watanabe provides an interesting description of the moral system that may have kept Santiago Chimaltenango from splintering during this period.

39. Zur 1998, 18.
40. Steiner (1961, 5) defined the sense of the tragic as: "the shortness of heroic life, the exposure of man to the murderousness and caprice of the inhuman, the fall of the City." Nacho's story fits this definition.
41. Turner (2000) and White (1987).
42. Renato Rosaldo 1989, 1–21, and Behar 1996, 34–89. See Rosenblatt, Walsh, and Jackson (1976) and Brison and Leavitt (1995) on cross-cultural patterns in grief and mourning.
43. Chodorow 1999.
44. See Spiro (1982) for the psychoanalytic view and Michelle Rosaldo (1983) and Catherine Lutz (1988) for the constructionist view.
45. Richardson 1975, 529–530.

Chapter 2

1. These figures are based on a census I did with the help of Nacho and a mestizo who got along very well with the Nahuat.
2. García Martínez (1987, 163–164, 169) found a colonial document, dated 1599, complaining of the Nahuat resistance to the Spanish colonial policy of congregation, or "congregación."
3. Schryer (1990, 63–66), Hill (1995), and Sandstrom (2000).

Chapter 3

1. Thomson 1991, 206.
2. Ibid., 207. Totonacs in and around nearby Papantla on the Gulf Coast also rose up in rebellion against the whites during the nineteenth century (Velasco 1979; Alvarado Sil 2005). However, the bloodiest rebellions took place in the Yucatan, where Alfonso Villa Rojas (1979, 50) estimated the death toll at around 300,000, and most were Mayans.
3. Thomson 1991, 207.
4. Ibid., 206.
5. See Brewster (2003) for an account of Gabriel Barrios and his cacicazgo.
6. See Stephen (2002, 44–50) for an account of how Emiliano Zapata's contribution to land redistribution became an important part of public school curricula during the presidency of Lázaro Cárdenas (1934–1940).
7. Victor Ballinas, "Se ocultó desde 1992 informe de la CNDH sobre 206 desaparaciones en Guerrero," online posting, July 1, 2001 <http://www.jornada.unam.mx/2001/jul01/010730/008n1pol.html>.
8. "Hasta ce viaje quintepayanqueh mil den quitocah. Nochi quipatqueh mil. Ompa quemah. Ihcuac peuhque cualayot. . . . Oncaya mauhcayot. Peuhqueh ya quinmimictiah. Peuhqueh ya quinixtacahuiquih. Peuqueh mopihpiyah ya. Mopihpiyah ihcon. Hasta que ihcon quintamictiyaqueh mas ahmo tei itahtacol. Quichtacamictiqueh."
9. "Yo estaba en Huitzilan. Guardo en mi memoria la entrada del ejército

al pueblo. Y la forma en que la familia Coyote se integra a la actividad esta de destruir la milpa. Haciendo uso, bueno, de la fuerza. De la fuerza. No hubo en este momento ningún muerto, ningún herido. Porque en este momento la UCI así bien tenía armas y hacía en algunos momentos gala de ellas. Las usía. Porque la gente se paseaba por las calles del pueblo con las armas encima. No se enfrentaron al ejército por supuesto que se hicieron bien. No se enfrentaron al ejército. Sin embargo se pusieron alguna resistencia digamos pacífica. Y el ejército sí tuvo que hacer uso de la fuerza para que ellos salieran de allí. No hiriendo a nadie pero. . . . Y la familia Coyote actuó con prepotencia, con burla de los sucedidos. Entiéndose triunfadora de los acontecimientos. Y a ellos se unieron, los más jóvenes de la familia, nietos de don Coyote y algunos otros muchachos que trabajaron para ellos entre ellos la familia de Wolf. Tres o cuatro jóvenes de esa familia. Que participaron activamente, físicamente estuvieron allí en el terreno cuando fue el desahuicio y la acción esa de tumbar la milpa, destruir el sembrado de milpa. Este fue el detonante. La indignación que este causó en el pueblo. Y el detonante para que se respondiera con la violencia que respondió la UCI."

10. "No a la impunidad," editorial, *La Jornada de Oriente,* March 15, 2004.

11. Ing. Homero Aguirre Enríquez, "XVII aniversario de Antorcha Campesina en Huitzilan, en la sierra norte del estado de Puebla," online posting, February 20, 2004 <http://www.antorchacampesina.org.mx/bolprensa01.htm>.

12. Schryer 1990, 194.

13. Ibid., 46.

14. Ibid., 47.

15. Ibid., 47–48.

16. Stoll 1993.

17. Manz 2005 (2004), 100–102, 107–108.

18. Knopp 1933.

19. Taggart 1997, 216.

20. Karttunen 1983, 39.

21. Taggart 1997 (1983), 207–208.

22. López Austin 1988 (1980), 297.

23. Sandstrom 1991.

24. Nash 2001, 1–2. See Higgins (2004, 74) on the influence of Adam Smith and David Ricardo.

Chapter 4

1. Colby and van den Berghe (1969, 157) described Ixil and Ladino relations in Guatemala as "highly segmental, functionally specific and instrumental" and "circumscribed by well-defined roles."

2. Key and Ritchie de Key 1953, 90.

3. Karttunen 1983, 256, 318.

4. López Austin 1988 (1980), 162.

5. Sandstrom 1991.

6. López Austin 1988 (1980), 162.

7. Good 2005.

8. "Marcha en Puebla para pedir la libertad de tres líderes," *Uno más Uno,* October 14, 1982.

9. "Falta de mercado al Café Poblano," *El Sol de Puebla,* December 8, 1982.

10. Sara Lovera and Luis A. Rodriguez, "La lucha electoral en Puebla reducida a 83 de 217 municipios," *Uno más Uno,* November 14, 1983.

11. Miyācaco means "Place of the Corn Tassel and Flower." It is a combination of miyāhuat = corn tassel and flower (Karttunen 1983, 149) and the locative suffice -co.

12. Evans-Pritchard 1980 (1976), 1.

13. Nacho had provided an example of such a rite during the earlier fieldwork. He told how a nahual advised a man who had lost a valuable object to burn seven loads of dry wood and seven loads of green wood in one chamber of a steam bath, or "temazcal," and then pour one liter of oil on the red-hot embers. The nahual then told the man to place an image of Saint Anthony, a saint renowned for finding lost objects, in a second chamber of the temazcal, into which he must also fan the steam produced by pouring oil on the embers in the first chamber. According to Nacho's story, the rite was efficacious because the thief died and the nahual's client recovered the stolen object. Nacho said a nahual can perform those rites successfully because he or she has a strong spirit and works with the devil, or ahmo cualli.

Chapter 5

1. Boas (1912) traced this story to Spain and Portugal.
2. Geertz 1977 (1973), 412–453.
3. Scott 1990, 163.
4. Beidelman 1961.
5. Scott 1990, 163.
6. Ibid., 162–165.
7. Ibid., 164.
8. Ibid.
9. Karttunen 1983, 218.
10. Graulich 1997. See Zerubavel (2003) on ways of reckoning time.
11. White 1987, 177.
12. On July 27, 2005.

Chapter 6

1. Karttunen 1983, 59, 253.
2. Quiñones Keber 1995, 29, 183.
3. López Austin 1997.
4. Graulich 1997, 46–56.
5. There are a number of accounts of the original transgression in Tamoan-

chan, and they mention different deities. See Graulich (1997, 55) for a list of the gods, their transgressions, and the consequences.

6. Graulich 1997, 58–59, and López Austin 1997, 100. López Austin (1997, 13) also noted that there are other accounts of the creation of the celestial and earthly realms, and they also draw attention to the role of the feminine; one, for example, tells of an "original monstrous, aquatic, chaotic goddess" that splits to create the masculine celestial realm and the feminine earthly one.

7. López Austin 1997, 13, 15.

8. Aramoni Burgete 1990, 177–178.

9. Graulich 1997, 46–56.

10. Galinier 1990, 623.

11. López Austin 1997, 154; Ichon 1973, 299.

12. Taggart 1997 (1983), 179.

13. Taggart 1975, 68–108.

14. See López Austin 1997, 154–155.

15. Aramoni Burgete (1990, 177–178) and Knab (1991) have described the use and the symbolism of the flower tree, or xochicuahuit, in other northern sierra of Puebla communities that Nacho did not mention. Among them is San Miguel Tzinacapan, near Cuetzalan (Knab 1991).

16. The meanings attached to the four cardinal directions are widespread in the northern sierra of Puebla (Taggart 1997 [1983]) and appear in the narratives of Nahuatl speakers in Tlaxcala (Hill 1995).

17. Karttunen 1983, 411.

18. Ibid., 243.

19. Mauss 1967, 19.

20. The Nahuat in general and Nacho in particular represented the sexuality of women differently than did the Spanish men in Brandes's (1980) careful study of expressive culture.

Chapter 7

1. "Toni ticchieutoc, nahueh?"

2. "Ay nahueh ya, ahmo xinechmaga . . . niquelnamictoc."

3. Karttunen 1983, 197.

4. Good 2005, 285–290.

5. Erysipelas is a disease caused by a hemolytic streptococcus and has the symptoms of a high fever and the accumulation of edema, a serumlike liquid, under local areas of the skin.

6. Leach 1968, 2.

7. Molina 1966, 346.

8. Chodorow 1999, 14. Alan Dundes (1987, 3–46) consistently argued that oral narrators project their deepest feelings stored in the unconscious into their narratives. The projections become apparent by carefully comparing their stories with cognate narratives told by storytellers in the same and in historically related cultures. See Taggart (1997 [1983], 1990, 1997). Michel de Certeau (1988 [1984],

xxi) also contends that readers project meanings into written texts. Projection, he wrote, "makes the text habitable, like a rented apartment. It transforms another person's property into a space borrowed for a moment by a transient."

Chapter 8

1. McKeever Furst 1995.
2. Taggart 1979, 1997 (1983).
3. Stoler (1995) and Limón (1998).
4. Freud 1975 (1905), 62, 64–65.
5. Karttunen 1983, 94.
6. Ibid., 220.
7. "Tacat quitazohta in cihuat. Yeh chocatinemia porque yeh quitazohtaya. Por eso quitemotinemia. In cihuat ahmo quitazohta in yoquich. Ahmo porque aquin quipiyah icnoyot de ome, parejo motazohtah. Huan ahmo ahuilchihuah."
8. "Huan como telcenca tiopanticalaquiah, pues iuhqui timonehnequeh ihuan nocihuauh catca, Victoria."
9. Karttunen 1983, 162.
10. Taggart 1997, 215–216.

Chapter 9

1. Nacho's 1970 Orpheus myth fits the pattern, noted by Fortes (1950) and Levi-Strauss (1963, 31–54), in which a strong brother-and-sister tie means a weak tie between husband and wife. However, his 1978 Orpheus myth reveals how that opposition disappeared as his courtship gave way to a solid marriage.
2. Karttunen 1983, 232.
3. Good 2005.
4. Malinowski 1929, 540–572.
5. Ibid., 572.
6. Spiro 1982, 78.
7. Moore 1964.
8. Bierhorst 1992, 34.
9. Coe and Whittaker 1982, 131–144.
10. Taggart 1986, 451–453.
11. Taggart 1992. The Nahuat images of the brother and sister resemble Romantic Period sculpture representing "Cupid and Psyche" as an adolescent brother and sister on the verge of feeling desire (Hagstrum 1977). Also, like some of the Romantic poets (Hagstrum 1977), Nacho, in his first Orpheus myth, had represented the sister and brother as sharing a pure kind of love. The sister did a good turn for her brother by trying to warn him that his wayward wife did not love him as he loved her.
12. As a "sister" she moved from being an outsider to an insider in his patrilineal extended family. Gilmore (2001, 226), using the work of Jean Jackson

(1996), contends that the outsider status of women who marry into such families contributes to the male malady of misogyny.

13. The Nahuat of Huitzilan refer to the embroidery as pehpenalō, which comes from the verb pehpena, meaning "to pick, choose someone, to gather, collect or glean something" (Karttunen 1983, 190). The noun pehpenalō refers to the act of embroidery, which looks like picking at a piece of cloth with a needle and thread.

14. "Motazohtayah, tanto in cihuat como tacat."

15. "Timotazohtayah. Quemmeh nehha como yehha, nechtazohtaya telcenca. Ahmo quemman nicmaga, nion yehha. Pues cualtzin timotazohtayah. Timoahhuayah. Nicahhuayo. Nechcahhuayo. Pero ompa za. Pero ahmo timotehuiayah."

16. Karttunen 1983, 219.

17. Ricoeur 2006 (2004), 95.

18. "Nehha nicmachilia que nictazohta porque nicmachiliaya tech noihtic, tech noyollo, que ahmo nicahcizquia occe cihuat ihcon. Ahmo oncaya occe cihuat quemeh yeh nechtazohtaya. Huan ihcon como yeh nechtazohtaya telcenca, ta ahmo nicncequia mah tehza cocoz. Ahmo nicnequia mah mayana. Ahmo nicnequia mah quicua quiera ce moyot. Nictazohtaya pero ca nochi noyollo."

19. "Ticmatiz que yeh nechtazohtaya porque ahmo tacuaya como ahmo (neh) tacuaz ihuan. Como nyahya Zacapoaxtla, mas niehco tapoyah, que nechchixtoc. Ahmo tacua. Zen ca neh tacuaz huan nohuan tacuaz. Como ahmo niehco, chocatoc. Que nechtemotoc. Como nyo mila, nechtematic que chocatic que yeh ahmo niehco. Por eso nicmachilia que nechtazohta."

20. Ricoeur 2006 (2004), 15–18.

21. Freud 1917.

22. Ibid., 244.

23. Scheper-Hughes 1992, 429–433.

24. Ibid., 359.

25. Abu-Lughod 1985. See also Nancy Chodorow (1978) for a theoretical account of why men and women in Western cultures might express emotions differently.

26. Woodrick 1995.

27. Zur 1998, 212.

28. Ibid., 12.

Chapter 10

1. Behar 1996, 85.
2. Ricoeur 2006 (2004), 99.
3. Ibid., 15, 18.
4. Ibid., 16, 17.
5. Ibid., 17.
6. Chodorow 1999, 14.
7. Geertz 1988, 43.
8. Bowlby 1969.

9. Scheper-Hughes 1992.

10. Freud 1989 (1961).

11. Counihan 1999. Ricoeur (2006 [2004], 16) credits Aristotle with associating the memory of feelings and bodily experience.

12. See Ricoeur (2006 [2004], 118) on the relationship between culture and collective memory.

13. Freud 1946 (1918).

14. Evans-Pritchard 1966 (1951), 52.

15. Fortes 1949, 98.

16. See Giddens (1992, 37–48) and Goody (1996, 184–187) for different views on the distribution of romantic love in time and space. See also Rosenblatt's (1967) summary of the ethnographic reports of romantic love around the world. Nevertheless, Laura Ahearn (2004) described in rich detail how courtship in Nepal changed with the introduction of Western romantic love. Oscar Lewis (1963 [1951], 400–401) found evidence of romantic love in love letters in the Nahuatl community of Tepoztlan in the 1940s.

17. Taggart 1990, 93–115.

18. Good 2005.

19. "Como yehha tequiti quittac cual tacat. Cual centequitih, no quitazohta, porque yeh quichieutoc de nen chihuazquia ahmo nihueli."

20. "Tehhan timomiliqueh que in tacat como ahmo in cihuat, ahmo pohcachihua. Huan igual cihuat. Como ahmo tacat, ahmo pohcachihua."

21. Freud 1914.

22. Freud 1989 (1961).

23. Gallop 1982, 22.

24. Burkhart 1996. The friars also introduced their idea of love when teaching about contrition (Burkhart 1989, 33).

25. Quezada 1975, 26–27; 1996.

26. Rosenfeld 1980, 20.

Works Cited

Abu-Lughod, Lila. 1985. "Honor and the Sentiments of Loss in a Bedouin Society." *American Ethnologist* 12 (2): 245–261.

Aguirre Enriquez, Ing. Homero. 2004. "XVII aniversario de Antorcha Campesina en Huitzilan, en la sierra norte del estado de Puebla." Online posting, February 20, 2004. <http://antorchacampesina.org.mx/bolprensa01.htm>

Ahearn, Laura M. 2004. *Invitations to Love: Literacy, Love Letters and Social Change in Nepal.* Ann Arbor: University of Michigan Press.

Alvarado Sil, Isis Marlene. 2005. "Repartimiento de mercancías y sublevación en Papantla, siglo XVIII." Tesis licenciado en etnohistoria. Escuela Nacional de Antropología e Historia.

Aramoni Burgete, María Elena. 1990. *Tlalokan Tata, Tlalokan Nana: Hierofanías y testimonios de un mundo indígena.* México: Consejo Nacional para la Cultura y las Artes.

Ballinas, Victor. 2001. "Se ocultó desde 1992 informe de la CNDH sobre 206 desapariciones en Guerrero." July 1. <http://www.jornada.unam.mx/2001/jul01/010730/008n1pol.html>

Behar, Ruth. 1996. *The Vulnerable Observer: Anthropology That Breaks Your Heart.* Boston: Beacon Press.

Beidelman, Thomas O. 1961. "Hyena and Rabbit: A Kaguru Representation of Matrilineal Relations." *Africa: Journal of the International African Institute* 31 (1): 61–74.

Bierhorst, John, trans. 1992. *History and Mythology of the Aztecs: The Codex Chimalpopoca.* Tucson: University of Arizona Press.

Boas, Franz. 1912. "Notes on Mexican Folk-Lore." *Journal of American Folklore* 25 (97): 204–260.

Bowlby, John. 1969. *Attachment.* New York: Basic Books.

Brandes, Stanley. 1980. *Metaphors of Masculinity: Sex and Status in Andalusian Folklore.* Philadelphia: University of Pennsylvania Press.

Brewster, Keith. 2003. *Militarism, Ethnicity, and Politics in the Sierra Norte de Puebla, 1917–1930.* Tucson: University of Arizona Press.

Briggs, Charles L. 1988. *Competence in Performance: The Creativity of Tradition in Mexicano Verbal Art.* Philadelphia: University of Pennsylvania Press.

Brison, Karen J., and Stephen C. Leavitt. 1995. "Coping with Bereavement: Long-Term Perspectives on Grief and Mourning." *Ethos* 23 (4): 395–400.

Burkhart, Louise M. 1989. *The Slippery Earth: Nahua-Christian Moral Dialogue in Sixteenth-Century Mexico*. Tucson: University of Arizona Press.

———. 1996. *Holy Wednesday: A Nahua Drama from Early Colonial Mexico*. Philadelphia: University of Pennsylvania Press.

Camahji, Alfredo. 1979. "Panorama de la lucha campesina 1977–1978." Estudios Políticos de la Facultad de Ciencas Políticas de la UNAM 1 February 1979: 1–11. Nexos, Sociedad, Ciencia y Literatura, S.A. de C.V. <http://web .lexis-nexis.com>

Chevalier, Jacques M., and Daniel Buckles. 1995. *A Land without Gods: Process Theory, Maldevelopment and the Mexican Nahuas*. London and Atlantic Highlands, N.J.: Zed Books.

Chodorow, Nancy. 1978. *The Reproduction of Mothering: Psychoanalysis and the Sociology of Gender*. Berkeley and Los Angeles: University of California Press.

———. 1999. *The Power of Feelings: Personal Meaning in Psychoanalysis, Gender and Culture*. New Haven, Conn.: Yale University Press.

Coe, Michael D., and Gordon Whittaker. 1982. *Aztec Sorcerers in Seventeenth Century Mexico: The Treatise on Superstitions by Hernando Ruiz de Alarcón*. Publication No. 7. Albany: Institute for Mesoamerican Studies, State University of New York at Albany.

Colby, Benjamin N., and Pierre L. van den Berghe. 1969. *Ixil Country: A Plural Society in Highland Guatemala*. Berkeley and Los Angeles: University of California Press.

Collier, George A., with Elizabeth Lowery Quaratiello. 1999 (1994). *Basta! Land and the Zapatista Rebellion in Chiapas*. New York: First Food Books.

Colson, Elizabeth. 1971. "Heroism, Martyrdom and Courage: An Essay on Tonga Ethics." In *The Translation of Culture: Essays to E. E. Evans-Pritchard*, ed. T. O. Beidelman, pp. 19–25. London: Tavistock.

Counihan, Carole. 1999. *The Anthropology of Food and Body*. New York: Routledge.

Crapanzano, Vincent. 1985 (1980). *Tuhami: A Portrait of a Moroccan*. Chicago: Chicago University Press.

de Certeau, Michel. 1988 (1984). *The Practice of Everyday Life*. Berkeley and Los Angeles: University of California Press.

Dundes, Alan. 1980. *The Morphology of North American Indian Folktales*. Helsinki: Suomalainen Tiedeakatemia.

———. 1987. *Parsing through Customs: Essays by a Freudian Folklorist*. Madison: University of Wisconsin Press.

Earle, Duncan, and Jeanne Simonelli. 2005. *Uprising of Hope: Sharing the Zapatista Journey to Alternative Development*. Walnut Creek, Calif.: Altamira Press.

El Sol de Puebla. 1982. "Falta de mercado al Café Poblano." *El Sol de Puebla*, December 8.

Evans-Pritchard, E. E. 1966 (1951). *Kinship and Marriage among the Nuer*. Oxford: Oxford University Press.

————. 1980 (1976). *Witchcraft, Oracles and Magic among the Azande.* Oxford: Clarendon Press.

Fortes, Meyer. 1949. *The Web of Kinship among the Tallensi: The Second Part of an Analysis of the Social Structure of a Trans-Volta Tribe.* London: Oxford University Press.

————. 1950. "Kinship and Marriage among the Ashanti." In *African Systems of Kinship and Marriage,* ed. A. R. Radcliffe-Brown and Daryll Forde, pp. 252–284. London: Oxford University Press.

Freud, Sigmund. 1914. "On Narcissism: An Introduction." In *The Standard Edition of the Complete Psychological Works of Sigmund Freud,* translated and edited by James Strachey, pp. 14:67–102. London: Hogarth Press and the Institute of Psychoanalysis.

————. 1917. "Mourning and Melancholia." In *The Standard Edition of the Complete Psychological Works of Sigmund Freud,* translated and edited by James Strachey, pp. 14:239–258. London: Hogarth Press and the Institute of Psychoanalysis.

————. 1933 (1932). "Femininity." In *The Standard Edition of the Complete Psychological Works of Sigmund Freud,* translated and edited by James Strachey, pp. 22:112–135. London: Hogarth Press and the Institute of Psychoanalysis.

————. 1946 (1918). *Totem and Taboo: Resemblances between the Psychic Lives of Savages and Neurotics.* New York: Vintage Books.

————. 1975 (1905). *Three Essays on the Theory of Sexuality.* New York: Basic Books.

————. 1989 (1961). *Civilization and Its Discontents.* New York: W. W. Norton.

Friedlander, Judith. 1975. *Being Indian in Hueyapan: A Study of Forced Identity in Contemporary Mexico.* New York: St. Martin's Press.

Galinier, Jacques. 1990. *La mitad del mundo: Cuerpo y cosmos en los rituales otomís.* México: UNAM/CEMCA/INI.

Gallop, Jane. 1982. *The Daughter's Seduction: Feminism and Psychoanalysis.* Ithaca, N.Y.: Cornell University Press.

García Martínez, Bernardo. 1987. *Los pueblos de la sierra: El poder y el espacio entre los indios del norte de Puebla hasta 1700.* México: Colegio de México.

Gayton, A. H. 1935. "The Orpheus Myth in North America." *Journal of American Folklore* 48 (189): 263–293.

Geertz, Clifford. 1977 (1973). *The Interpretation of Cultures.* New York: Basic Books.

————. 1988. *Works and Lives: The Anthropologist as Author.* Stanford, Calif.: Stanford University Press.

Giddens, Anthony. 1992. *The Transformation of Intimacy: Sexuality, Love and Eroticism in Modern Societies.* Stanford, Calif.: Stanford University Press.

Gilmore, David D. 2001. *Misogyny: The Male Malady.* Philadelphia: University of Pennsylvania Press.

Good, Catherine. 2005. "'Trabajando juntos como uno': Conceptos nahuas del grupo doméstico y de la persona." In *Familia y parentesco en México y Mesoamérica: Unas miradas antropológicas,* ed. David Robichaux, pp. 275–294. México: Universidad Iberoamericana, A. C.

Goody, Jack. 1996. *The East in the West*. Cambridge: Cambridge University Press.

Gossen, Gary H. 1994. "From Olmecs to Zapatistas: A Once and Future History of Souls." *American Anthropologist* 96 (3): 553–570.

Graulich, Michel. 1997. *Myths of Ancient Mexico*. Norman: University of Oklahoma Press.

Green, Linda. 1999. *Fear as a Way of Life: Mayan Widows in Rural Guatemala*. New York: Columbia University Press.

Guiteras Holmes, Calixta. 1965. *Los peligros del alma: Visión del mundo de un tzotzil*. México: Fondo de Cultura Económica.

Hagstrum, Jean H. 1977. "Eros and Psyche: Some Versions of Romantic Love and Delicacy." *Critical Inquiry* 3 (3): 521–542.

Harkin, Michael Eugene. 2003. "Feeling and Thinking in Memory and Forgetting: Toward an Ethnohistory of Emotions." *Ethnohistory* 50 (2): 261–284.

Higgins, Nicholas P. 2004. *Understanding the Chiapas Rebellion: Modernist Visions and the Invisible Indian*. Austin: University of Texas Press.

Hill, Jane. 1995. "The Voices of Don Gabriel: Responsibility and Self in a Modern Mexican Narrative." In *The Dialogic Emergence of Culture*, ed. Dennis Tedlock and Bruce Mannheim, pp. 97–147. Urbana: University of Illinois Press.

Hultkrantz, Åke. 1957. *The North American Indian Orpheus Tradition: A Contribution to Comparative Religion*. Publication no. 8. Stockholm: Statens Etnografiska Museum.

Ichon, Alain. 1973. *La religión de los totonacas de la Sierra*. México: Instituto Nacional Indigenista.

Ingham, John. 1986. *Mary, Michael, and Lucifer: Folk Catholicism in Central Mexico*. Austin: University of Texas Press.

Jackson, Jean E. 1996. "Coping with the Dilemmas of Affinity and Female Sexuality: Male Rebirth in the Central Northwest Amazon." In *Denying Biology: Essays on Gender and Pseudo-Procreation*, ed. Warren Shapiro and Uli Linke, pp. 89–127. Lanham, Md.: University Press of America.

James, Wendy. 1997. "The Names of Fear: Memory, History, and the Ethnography of Feeling among Uduk Refugees." *Journal of the Royal Anthropological Institute* 3 (1): 115–131.

Karttunen, Frances. 1983. *An Analytical Dictionary of Nahuatl*. Austin: University of Texas Press.

Kellogg, Susan. 1995. *Law and the Transformation of Aztec Culture, 1500–1700*. Norman: University of Oklahoma Press.

Kenny, Michael G. 1999. "A Place for Memory: The Interface between Individual and Collective History." *Comparative Studies in Society and History* 41 (3): 420–437.

Key, Harold, and Mary Ritchie de Key. 1953. *Vocabulario mejicano de la Sierra de Zacapoaxtla, Puebla*. México: Instituto Lingüístico de Verano/la Dirección General de Asuntos Indígenas de la Secretaría de Educación Pública.

Knab, Tim J. 1991. "Geografía del Inframundo." *Estudios de Cultura Nahuatl* 21: 31–57.

Knopp, Grace. 1933. "The Motifs of the 'Jason and Medea Myth' in Modern

Tradition (A Study of Märchentypus 313)." Ph.D. diss. submitted to the Department of Romance Languages of Stanford University.

La Jornada de Oriente Editor. 2004. "No a la impunidad." *La Jornada de Oriente*, March 15.

Langness, L. L., and Geyla Frank. 1981. *Lives: An Anthropological Approach to Biography*. Novato, Calif.: Chandler and Sharp.

Laughlin, Robert M. 1962. "Through the Looking Glass: Reflections on Zinacantan Courtship and Marriage." Ph.D. diss., Harvard University.

Leach, E. R. 1968. "Introduction." In *Dialectic in Practical Religion*, ed. E. R. Leach, pp. 1–6. London: Cambridge University Press.

León Portilla, Miguel. 1970 (1964). *El reverso de la conquista*. México: Editorial Joaquín Mortiz.

Levallé, Bernard. 1999. *Amor y opresión en los Andes coloniales*. Lima: Instituto Francés de Estudios Andinos.

Levi-Strauss, Claude. 1963. *Structural Anthropology*. New York: Basic Books.

Lewis, Oscar. 1949. "Husbands and Wives in a Mexican Village: A Study of Role Conflict." *American Anthropologist* 51 (4): 602–611.

———. 1963 (1951). *Life in a Mexican Village: Tepoztlán Restudied*. Urbana: University of Illinois Press.

———. 1967 (1964). *Pedro Martínez: A Mexican Peasant and His Family*. New York: Vintage.

Limón, José Eduardo. 1998. *American Encounters: Greater Mexico and the Erotics of Culture*. Boston: Beacon Press.

Lockhart, James. 1992. *The Nahuas after the Conquest: A Social and Cultural History of the Indians of Central Mexico, Sixteenth through Eighteenth Centuries*. Stanford, Calif.: Stanford University Press.

López Austin, Alfredo. 1988 (1980). *The Human Body and Ideology: Concepts of the Ancient Nahuas*. Vol. 1. Salt Lake City: University of Utah Press.

———. 1997. *Tamoanchan, Tlalocan: Places of Mist*. Niwot: University Press of Colorado.

Lovera, Sara, and Luis A. Rodriguez. 1983. "La lucha electoral en Puebla, reducida a 83 de 217 municipios." *Uno más Uno*, November 14.

Lurie, Nancy O. 1966 (1961). *Mountain Wolf Woman, Sister of Crashing Thunder: The Autobiography of a Winnebago Indian*. Ann Arbor: University of Michigan Press.

Lutz, Catherine. 1988. *Unnatural Emotions: Everyday Sentiments on a Micronesian Atoll and Their Challenge to Western Theory*. Chicago: University of Chicago Press.

McKeever Furst, Jill. 1995. *The Natural History of the Soul in Ancient Mexico*. New Haven, Conn.: Yale University Press.

Malinowski, Bronislaw. 1929. *The Sexual Life of Savages in North-Western Melanesia: An Ethnographic Account of Courtship, Marriage and Family Life among the Natives of the Trobriand Islands, British New Guinea*. New York: Harcourt, Brace and World.

Manz, Beatríz. 2005 (2004). *Paradise in Ashes: A Guatemalan Journey of Courage, Terror, and Hope*. Berkeley and Los Angeles: University of California Press.

Marx, Karl. 1964. *The Economic and Philosophic Manuscript of 1844.* New York: International Publishers.

Mauss, Marcel. 1967. *The Gift: Forms and Functions of Exchange in Archaic Societies.* New York: W. W. Norton.

Molina, Fray Alonso de. 1966. *Vocabulario Nahuatl-Castellano, Castellano-Nahuatl.* México: Ediciones Colofon, S. A.

Moore, Sally F. 1964. "Descent and Symbolic Filiation." *American Anthropologist* 66 (6): 1308–1320.

Nash, June. 1997. "Gendered Deities and the Survival of Culture." *History of Religions* 36 (4): 333–356.

———. 2001. *Mayan Visions: The Quest for Autonomy in an Age of Globalization.* New York: Routledge.

Pitt-Rivers, J. A. 1966. *The People of the Sierra.* Chicago: Chicago University Press.

Quezada, Noemí. 1975. *Amor y magia amorosa entre los aztecas: supervivencia en el México colonial.* México: Instituto de Investigaciones Antropológicas, Universidad Autónoma de México.

———. 1996. *Sexualidad, amor, y eroticismo: México prehispánico y México colonial.* México: Universidad Autónoma de México.

Quiñones Keber, Eloise. 1995. *Codex Telleriano-Remensis: Ritual, Divination, and History in a Pictorial Aztec Manuscript.* Austin: University of Texas Press.

Radin, Paul. 1926. *Crashing Thunder: The Autobiography of an American Indian.* New York and London: D. Appleton and Company.

Richardson, Miles. 1975. "Anthropologist—The Myth Teller." *American Ethnologist* 2: 517–533.

Ricoeur, Paul. 2006 (2004). *Memory, History, Forgetting.* Chicago: Chicago University Press.

Rosaldo, Michelle Z. 1983. "The Shame of Headhunters and the Autonomy of Self." *Ethos* 11 (3): 135–151.

Rosaldo, Renato. 1989. *Culture and Truth: The Remaking of Social Analysis.* Boston: Beacon Press.

Rosenblatt, Paul. C. 1967. "Marital Residence and the Functions of Romantic Love." *Ethnology* 6 (4): 471–480.

Rosenblatt, Paul C., R. Patricia Walsh, and Douglas A. Jackson. 1976. *Grief and Mourning in Cross-Cultural Perspective.* New Haven, Conn.: HRAF Press.

Rosenfeld, Alvin H. 1980. *A Double Dying: Reflections on Holocaust Literature.* Bloomington: Indiana University Press.

Rovira, Guimar. 2002. "Of Love, Marriage, Children and War." In *The Zapatista Reader,* ed. Tom Hayden, pp. 452–471. New York: Thunder's Mouth Press/Nation Books.

Sandstrom, Alan. 1991. *Corn Is Our Blood: Culture and Ethnic Identity in a Contemporary Aztec Indian Village.* Norman: University of Oklahoma Press.

———. 2000. "Toponymic Groups and House Organization: The Nahuas of Northern Veracruz, Mexico." In *Beyond Kinship: Social and Material Reproduction in House Societies,* ed. Rosemary A. Joyce and Susan D. Gillespie, pp. 53–72. Philadelphia: University of Pennsylvania Press.

————. in press. "Blood Sacrifice, Curing, and Ethnic Identity among Contemporary Nahua of Mexico." In *Ethnic Identity in Indigenous Mesoamerica: The View from Archaeology, Art History, Ethnohistory, and Contemporary Ethnography*, ed. Francs F. Berdan, John K. Chance, Alan R. Sandstrom, Barbara L. Stark, James Taggart, and Emily Umberger. Salt Lake City: University of Utah Press.

Scheper-Hughes, Nancy. 1992. *Death without Weeping: The Violence of Everyday Life in Brazil*. Berkeley and Los Angeles: University of California Press.

————. 1996. "Small Wars and Invisible Genocides." *Social Science and Medicine* 43 (5): 889–900.

Schryer, Frans J. 1990. *Ethnicity and Class Conflict in Rural Mexico*. Princeton, N.J.: Princeton University Press.

Scott, James C. 1990. *Domination and the Arts of Resistance*. New Haven, Conn.: Yale University Press.

Sherzer, Joel. 1983. *Kuna Ways of Speaking*. Austin: University of Texas Press.

Spiro, Melford. 1982. *Oedipus in the Trobriands*. Chicago: University of Chicago Press.

Steiner, George. 1961. *The Death of Tragedy*. New York: Alfred A. Knopf.

Stephen, Lynn. 2002. *¡Zapata Lives! Histories and Cultural Politics in Southern Mexico*. Berkeley and Los Angeles: University of California Press.

Stoler, Ann Laura. 1995. *Race and the Education of Desire: Foucault's History of Sexuality and the Colonial Order of Things*. Durham, N.C.: Duke University Press.

Stoll, David. 1993. *Between Two Armies in the Ixil Towns of Guatemala*. New York: Columbia University Press.

Swanson, Guy E. 1976. "Orpheus and Star Husband: Meaning and the Structure of Myths." *Ethnology* 15 (2): 115–133.

Taggart, James M. 1975. *Estructura de los grupos domésticos de una comunidad de habla nahuat de Puebla*. México: Instituto Nacional Indigenista.

————. 1979. "Men's Changing Image of Women in Nahuat Oral Tradition." *American Ethnologist* 6 (4): 723–741.

————. 1986. "'Hansel and Gretel' in Spain and Mexico." *Journal of American Folklore* 99 (394): 435–460.

————. 1990. *Enchanted Maidens: Gender Relations in Spanish Folktales of Courtship and Marriage*. Princeton, N.J.: Princeton University Press.

————. 1992. "Gender Segregation and Cultural Constructions of Sexuality in Two Hispanic Societies." *American Ethnologist* 19 (1): 75–96.

————. 1997. *The Bear and His Sons: Masculinity in Spanish and Mexican Folktales*. Austin: University of Texas Press.

————. 1997 (1983). *Nahuat Myth and Social Structure*. Austin: University of Texas Press.

Taussig, Michael T. 1980. *The Devil and Commodity Fetishism in South America*. Chapel Hill: University of North Carolina Press.

Thomson, Guy P. C. 1991. "Agrarian Conflict in the Municipality of Cuetzalán (Sierra de Puebla): The Rise and Fall of 'Pala' Agustín Dieguillo, 1861–1894." *Hispanic American Historical Review* 71 (2): 205–258.

Turner, Jonathan H. 2000. *On the Origins of Human Emotions: A Sociological Inquiry into the Evolution of Human Affect.* Chicago: University of Chicago Press.

Vansina, Jan. 1985. *Oral Tradition as History.* Madison: University of Wisconsin Press.

Velasco Toro, José. 1979. "Indigenismo y rebelión totonaca de Papantala, 1885-. 1896." *América Indígena* 39: 81–105.

Villa Rojas, Alfonso. 1979. "Fieldwork in the Mayan Region of Mexico." In *Long-Term Field Research in Social Anthropology,* ed. George M. Foster, Thayer Scudder, Elizabeth Colson, and Robert V. Kemper, pp. 45–64. New York: Academic Press.

Watanabe, John M. 1992. *Maya Saints and Souls in a Changing World.* Austin: University of Texas Press.

Weisman, Gary. 2004. *Fantasies of Witnessing: Postwar Efforts to Experience the Holocaust.* Ithaca, N.Y.: Cornell University Press.

White, Hayden. 1987. *The Content of the Form: Narrative Discourse and Historical Representations.* Baltimore: Johns Hopkins University Press.

Woodrick, Anne C. 1995. "A Lifetime of Mourning: Grief Work among Yucatec Maya Woman." *Ethos* 23 (4): 401–423.

Zerubavel, Eviatar. 2003. *Time Maps: Collective Memory and the Social Shape of the Past.* Chicago: University of Chicago Press.

Zur, Judith. 1998. *Violent Memories: Mayan War Widows in Guatemala.* Boulder, Colo.: Westview Press.

Index

Abu-Lughod, Lila, 112, 127n25 (ch. 9)
Aco Cortés, Irene, 10
act big (hueichihua): and icnoyot (respect), 54; meaning of, 54–55
"Adam and Eve," 75
A Farewell to Arms, 116–117
Aguirre Enriquez, Ing. Homero, 123n11 (ch. 3)
Agustin Dieguillo, Pala, 36
Ahearn, Laura, 128n16 (ch. 10)
Alvarado Sil, Isis Marlene, 122n2 (ch. 3)
ancestors, 71
anger, 114; bodily center of, 5; erupting in Huitzilan, 2; Nacho's comments on, 72. *See also* cualayot
Annals of Cuauhtitlan, 107
Antorcha Campesina: arrival of, 56–57; Nacho's father-in-law killed by, 22; UCI dislodged by, 66; violence described by, 44
Aramoni Burgete, Maria Elena, 125nn8,15 (ch. 6)
Aristotle, 113
arms, source of, 48–49
army, 26
attachment, 114
Azande, 62

Balinese cockfight, and "Rabbit and Coyote," 65
Ballinas, Victor, 122n7 (ch. 3)

baptism, ritual of, 2. *See also* flower tree; xochicuahuit
Barrios, Gabriel, 38, 66
Behar, Ruth, 10, 113, 122n42 (ch. 1), 127n1 (ch. 10)
Beidelman, Thomas O., 124n4 (ch. 5)
Bierhorst, John, 126n8 (ch. 9)
"Blancaflor" (Tale Type 313C): image of earth in, 46; Nacho's images of women in, 102–103; nahueh in, 84
Boas, Franz, 124n1 (ch. 5)
Bowlby, John, 114, 127n8 (ch. 10)
Brandes, Stanley, 125n20 (ch. 6)
Brewster, Keith, 122n5 (ch. 3)
Briggs, Charles, 120n11 (ch. 1)
Brison, Karen J., 122n42 (ch. 1)
brothers: Nahuat term for, 53; teaching respect among, 53
Buckles, Daniel, 121n31 (ch. 1)
Burkhart, Louise, 117, 128n24 (ch. 10)

Cabañas, Lucio, UCI song extolling, 43
cacique. *See* Barrios, Gabriel
Calyecapan, 12, 65, 82; location of, 11; meaning of, 11; Nacho's home in, 83
Camahji, Alfredo, 121n33 (ch. 1)
Cárdenas, Lázaro, 44, 122n6 (ch. 3)
cardinal directions, ritual represent-

ing, 80. *See also* quadrilateral view
of the universe
ceremonial center, Huiztilan as,
79–80
Chachaloyan, ejido in, 40
Chevalier, Jacques M., 121n31 (ch. 1)
Chodorow, Nancy, 122n43 (ch. 1),
125n8 (ch. 7), 127n25 (ch. 9),
127n6 (ch. 10); on personal histories, 10; transference, defined by,
94, 113–114
chronology, 58–59
cihuat ahuilnemi, meaning of, 99–100
cihuatanqueh (intermediary), 81
Cihuatepet, 12, 85, 86
Cinteotl, 6, 74
class, and ethnicity, 44
Codex Telleriano Remensis, 73
Coe, Michael D., 126n9 (ch. 9)
Colby, Benjamin N., 123n1 (ch. 4)
collective memory, 110; grief in,
109–111; love in, 115; and Orpheus
tales, 115; and personal memory,
114; rituals of, 115
Collier, George A., 121n34 (ch. 1)
Colson, Elizabeth, 119n7 (ch. 1)
communalism, Nahuat conception
of, 6
communalistic culture, 6
compadrazgo, breaking of, 41
compassion, and suffering, 87. *See
also* teicneliliz
CONASUPO, definition of, 26
conception, Nahuat idea of, 47
congregación, Nahuat resistance to,
11
contraception, Victoria's use of, 108
corn: Nacho sharing, 35; strength
(chicahualiz) made by, 47
cornfields, chopping down, 46
corn plant: chopping down of, 43,
46–47; mythic origin of, 2
Counihan, Carole, 114, 128n11
(ch. 10)
courtship, Nacho's account of, 13–14
Coyote: and chopping down the
Talcuaco cornfield, 43; coveting

Metzancuauhtah, 70; as enemy
of UCI, 14–15; and "Rabbit and
Coyote," 15; as pseudonym, 14;
Rake's quarrel with, 39; Tlacuaco,
grabbed by, 14
Crapanzanzo, Vincent, 119n9 (ch. 1)
Crashing Thunder, 120n10 (ch. 1)
cualayot (anger), 114; erupting in
Huiztilan, 2; Nacho's account of,
15, 43; spark igniting, 46; as unfas-
tening, 81
cualtacayot (human goodness), 73,
75, 82
Cuetzalan del Progreso, Juana Gutierrez, originating from, 36
"Cupid and Psyche," 126n11 (ch. 9)

dead: land of, 99; number of, 44
de Certeau, Michel, 125n8 (ch. 7)
desire: in courtship, 116; Nahuat
expression for, 99; Nahuat theory
of, 5
disrespectful person (ilapac), qualities of, 92
Dog: and his relationship with
Nacho, 53–54; quarrelling with
Wolf, 39
Dundes, Alan, 125n8 (ch. 7)

Earle, Duncan, 121n31 (ch. 1)
earth, personification of, 46
Echeverría, Luis (1970–1976), 44
EGP (Ejército Guerrillero de los Po-
bres), 45
El Sol de Puebla, 124n9 (ch. 4)
emotion: approach to, 3–6, 9–10,
120n10 (ch. 1); bodily centers of,
4–5; as concept in recollection, 5;
and heart (yollo), 5; and liver (elli),
5; ritual construction of, 75; strong
(ilihuiz), 5. *See also* cualayot; cualtacayot; mauhcayot; tazohtaliz;
teicneliliz
Epifania: death of mother described
by, 61–62; grief for mother described by, 28–30; photo of, 29
Eros, 114

Erysipelas, 125n5 (ch. 7)
ethnicity, and class, 44
Evans-Pritchard, E. E., 115, 124n12
    (ch. 4), 128n14 (ch. 10)
exchange. *See* food
exodus, Nacho's account of, 25–27
EZLN (Ejército Zapatista de Liber-
    ación Nacional), 8

fear, 72. *See also* mauhcayot
federales, pursuing UCI, 14
Felipe Reyes: as radio novella charac-
    ter, 14, 39–40; shooting of, 14, 43;
    as UCI leader, 2, 9
flower necklace, 73, 85. *See also*
    xochicozcat
flower tree, 73, 80; and "Adam and
    Eve," 75; meaning of, 75; Nacho's
    interpretation of, 77–79; origin
    of, 73–74; photo of, 74. *See also*
    xochicuahuit
folktales. *See* "Blancaflor" (Tale Type
    313C); "Orpheus" (Tale Type
    400); "Rabbit and Coyote" (Tale
    Type 175 + 34)
food: ritual exchange of, 78, 81;
    sharing of, 52; and women, 6
Fortes, Meyer, 115, 126n1 (ch. 9),
    128n15 (ch. 10)
Frank, Geyla, 120n10 (ch. 10)
fratricide, 8. *See also* cualayot *and
    Chapter* 4
Freud, Sigmund, 111, 114, 116–117,
    126n4 (ch. 8), 127nn21,22 (ch. 9),
    128nn10,13,21,22 (ch. 10)
Friedlander, Judith, 121nn31,36
    (ch. 1)

Galinier, Jacques, 125n10 (ch. 6)
Gallop, Jane, 116, 128n23 (ch. 10)
García Martínez, Bernardo, 11, 122n2
    (ch. 2)
Gayton, A. H., 119n8 (ch. 1)
Geertz, Clifford, 65, 114, 124n2
    (ch. 5), 127n7 (ch. 10)
gender: hierarchy, 7; relations, 7, 41
Giddens, Anthony, 128n16 (ch. 10)

Gift, The, 81
Gilmore, David D., 126n12 (ch. 9)
globalization, definition of, 120–
    121n29 (ch. 1)
Good, Catherine, 87, 116, 123n7
    (ch. 4), 125n4 (ch. 7), 126n3
    (ch. 9), 128n17 (ch. 10); on love
    and work, 55
goodness. *See* cualtacayot
Goody, Jack, 128n16 (ch. 10)
Gossen, Gary H., 6, 120n27 (ch. 1)
Graulich, Michel, viii, 71, 73, 120n25
    (ch. 1), 124n10 (ch. 5), 124n4
    (ch. 6), 125nn5,6,9 (ch. 6)
Green, Linda, 9, 121nn37,38 (ch. 1)
grief: Nacho's description of, 23–24,
    110; Nahuat word for, 120n20
    (ch. 1); in "Orpheus," 109–110
Guiteras Holmes, Calixta, 120n17
    (ch. 1)
Gutierrez, Juana, 36–37

Hagstrum, Jean H., 126n11 (ch. 9)
Harkin, Michael Eugene, 120n10
    (ch. 1)
hate, Nahuat word for, 53
heart, as emotional center, 5
Hemingway, Ernest, 116–117
Hernández, Bartolomé, 86
Hernández, Domingo, 86
Higgins, Nicholas P., 121n36 (ch. 1),
    123n24 (ch. 3)
Hill, Jane, 122n3 (ch. 2), 125n16
    (ch. 6)
Holocaust, 119n5 (ch. 1)
Holy Wednesday, 117
Hopi, 7
horse, as bad omen, 23
Huahuaxtla, 80
Huasteca of Hidalgo, land invasions
    in, 8, 44
Huejutla, 8, 44
Hueyapan, 121n36 (ch. 1)
Huitzilan, 11–12
Hultkrantz, 119n8 (ch. 1)
human goodness, 73; ritual construc-
    tion of, 75. *See also* cualtacayot

Ichon, Alain, 125n11 (ch. 6)

icniuh (sibling), as prohibited object, 104

icnoyot (respect): Nacho's meaning of, 102; Nahuat definition of, 91–92; qualities of, 92; respeto and, 52; ritual spreading of, 2; sharing food and, 52; teaching of, 92–93

ilapac (disrespectful person), 92

incense carrier. *See* tapopoxhuiqueh

incest, Nahuat rule of, 104

Ingham, John, 121n31 (ch. 1)

Jackson, Douglas A., 122n42 (ch. 1)

Jackson, Jean E., 126–127n12 (ch. 9)

James, Wendy, 120n21 (ch. 1); emotion as concept, 5

Jimenez Morales, Guillermo, 57

Jornada, La, 44, 123n10 (ch. 3)

Justice of the Peace, duties of, 15

Karttunen, Frances, 101, 102, 119n3 (ch. 1), 120n12 (ch. 1), 123n19 (ch. 3), 123n3 (ch. 4), 124n11 (ch. 4), 124n9 (ch. 5), 124n1 (ch. 6), 125nn17,18 (ch. 6), 125n3 (ch. 7), 126nn5,6,9 (ch. 8), 126n2 (ch. 9), 127nn13,16 (ch. 9)

Kellogg, Susan, 121n31 (ch. 1)

Kenny, Michael G., 119nn5,9 (ch. 1)

Key, Harold, 53, 123n2 (ch. 4)

K'iche widows, 112

kinship, Nahuat conception of, 53–54

Knab, Tim J., 125n15 (ch. 6)

Knopp, Grace, 123n18 (ch. 3)

land, 40

land invasions, 2; Huasteca of Hidalgo, in, 8; Huitzilan, in, 8; number of, 8; Pepeyocatitla, in, 44

land pressure, effects of, 41

Langness, L. L., 120n10 (ch. 1)

Laughlin, Robert, 119n6 (ch. 1)

Leach, E. R., 125n6 (ch. 7)

Leavitt, Stephen C., 122n42 (ch. 1)

León Portilla, Miguel, 120n10 (ch. 1)

Levallé, Bernard, 121n31 (ch. 1)

Levi, Primo, 119n5 (ch. 1); on testimony, 30

Levi-Strauss, Claude, 126n1 (ch. 9)

Lewis, Oscar, 121n31 (ch. 1), 128n16 (ch. 10)

Limón, José, 126n3 (ch. 8)

liver (elli), as emotional center, 5

localities in Huitzilan. *See* Calyecapan; Metzancuauhtah; Miyacaco; Talcez; Talcuaco; Taltempan; Taltzintan; Xinachapan

López Austin, Alfredo, 47, 54, 73–75, 120nn15–17 (ch. 1), 123n22 (ch. 3), 123nn4,6 (ch. 4), 124nn3,6,7 (ch. 6), 125nn11,14 (ch. 6); on emotion and the body, 4–5

loss, 114

love: brother and sister, 126n11 (ch. 9); as desire, 99; Nacho felt for Victoria, 110–111; Nacho felt from mother, 86–87; Nacho felt from Victoria, 110; Nahua and Spanish conceptions of, 5; and work (tequit), 116. *See also* tazohtaliz

Lovera, Sara, 124n10 (ch. 4)

Lurie, Nancy, 120n10 (ch. 1)

Lutz, Catherine, 122n44 (ch. 1)

Malinowski, Bronislaw, 107, 126nn4,5 (ch. 9)

Mantz, Beatríz, 45, 123n17 (ch. 3)

marriage: love in, 115; Nahuat conception of, 99; Nahuat word for, 104. *See also Chapter 6*

Martínez, Gonzalo, 16

massacre: description of, 24; Epifania's account of, 61–62; explanation of, 62–64; mestizo account of, 60–61; Nacho's account of, 24–25

matrilocality, 86

mauhcayot (fear), Nacho's comments on, 72

Mauss, Marcel, 81, 125n19 (ch. 6)

McKeever Furst, Jill, 126n1 (ch. 8)

Medea, as Blancaflor, 46
melancholia, symptoms of, 111
memory, 119n8 (ch. 1); approach to,
  3–4; Nahuat word for, 3, 119n3
  (ch. 1); and narrative, 3; as passion,
  113; as recollection, 113; and transference, 113. *See also* Ricoeur,
  Paul
Mesoamerica, 6
mestizos: disputes among, 39; ethnicity marked by, 37; loss of power
  of, 66; Nahuat conception of, 99;
  number of, 40
Metzancuauhtah, 70
Miyacaco, 61, 114; meaning of,
  124n11 (ch. 4)
Molina, Fray Alonso de, 4, 91,
  120nn12,13 (ch. 1), 125n7 (ch. 7)
monism, Nahuat conception of, 47
Moore, Sally Falk, 126n7 (ch. 9)
mountains, gender of, 12
Mountain Wolf Woman, 120n10
  (ch. 1)
mourning, 111
"Mourning and Melancholia," 111

Nacho: ancestral home of, 12; anger
  interpreted by, 72; bad omen heard
  by, 23; and brother's death, 88; as
  caught in the middle, 15; children
  of, 23–24, 25; courtship of, 102;
  current home of, 12; Dog, relationship with, 53–54; extended family
  household of, 32–35, 83; father-
  in-law of, 17–18; father-in-law's
  death described by, 59–60; father
  of, 86, 88; father's death described
  by, 88; grief described by, 23, 110;
  Huitzilan, leaving, 22; as justice of
  the peace, 15–16; love for Victoria
  felt by, 110; love from Victoria felt
  by, 110–111; marriage described
  by, 109; massacre explained by,
  24–25; mother of, 83, 86; mother's
  death described by, 93–94;
  mother's love described by, 86;
  "Rabbit and Coyote" explained

by, 71–72; "Rabbit and Coyote"
  told by, 67–69; remarriage of,
  30–32; returning to Huitzilan,
  27–28; saved by Victoria, 111;
  schooling of, 88–89; shares corn
  with children, 35; shares traits with
  mother, 32–33; survivors, learning
  about, 24; taking children to Zacapoaxtla, 25–27; telling why father-
  in-law joined UCI, 17–18; was on
  UCI hit list, 16; women, representing in stories, 102–103; working
  as young man, 89–90; working in
  Mexico City, 22; Wrath attempted
  to kill, 18–22
nahual (witch), 63; rites by, 124n13
  (ch. 4). *See also* witchcraft
Nahuat, 1; disputes among, 39; location of the speakers of, 120n14
  (ch. 1); Nahuatl, difference from,
  120n12 (ch. 1); number of, 40;
  splintering of, 41
Nahuatl: location of speakers of,
  120n14 (ch. 1); Nahuat, difference
  from, 120n12 (ch. 1)
nahueh, 104; as Blancaflor, 84; linguistic derivation of, 85; meanings
  of, 83–84; as term for mother, 83.
  See also Chapter 7
Nanahuatzin, 80
nanahui, 78, 84; Nacho's explanation
  of, 79; photo of, 79; and quadrilateral view of the universe, 80
narration, 2
narrative, 3. *See also* neixcuitil
Nash, June, 47, 120n28 (ch. 1),
  123n24 (ch. 3); globalization, defined by, 120n29 (ch. 1)
neixcuitil, 3
Nuer, 115

Ometeotl, 73
"Orpheus" (Tale Type 400), 104;
  as anticipating experience, 4; as
  collective memory, 115; texts of,
  96–98, 105–107
Orpheus tradition, 119n8 (ch. 1)

Pahuatla, 80; jailed leaders from, 57;
UCI in, 8, 39
Pepeyocatitla: land invasion in, 44–
45, 121n33 (ch. 1)
personal histories, importance of, 9
personal memory, and collective
memory, 114
personhood: Mesoamerican conception of, 6–7; and style of narration, 6
Pitt-Rivers, J. A., 120n23 (ch. 1)
planting, symbolism of, 46
population, of mestizos in Huitzilan/
of Nahuat in Huitzilan, 11
post-partum sex taboo, 108
PRI, Nacho on slate of, 15
projection, 125–126n8 (ch. 7)
protagonists, list of, 38–39
Protestantism, conversion to, 41
PSUM (Partido Socialista Unificado
Mexicano), 57

quadrilateral view of the universe, 84;
and nahnahui, 80
Quaratiello, Elizabeth Lowery,
121n34 (ch. 1)
Quezada, Noemí, 7, 120n24 (ch. 1),
128n25 (ch. 10); on Spanish and
Nahua conceptions of love, 5
Quiñones Keber, Eloise, 119, 120n25
(ch. 1), 124n2 (ch. 6)

"Rabbit and Coyote" (Tale Type 175
+ 34): angry woman (tahuel cihuat)
in, 69; and Balinese cockfight, 65;
"Brer Rabbit," parallels to, 70;
changing meaning of, 70–72; and
Coyote as enemy of the UCI, 15; as
metaphor, 65; Nacho's exegesis of,
70–72; popularity of, 65; text of,
67–69; violence in, 66
Radin, Paul, 120n10 (ch. 1)
rage, erupting in Huitzilan, 2. See also
cualayot
rain gods (quiyauhteomeh), 80
Rake: and dispute with Coyote, 39;
as father of sixty children, 15; as
town hall president, 15

Ramirez, as Wolf's half brother, 14
Remembering Victoria, process of
writing, 10
respect: between mestizos and
Nahuat, 52; Nacho's meaning of,
102; Nahuat definition of, 91–92;
qualities of, 92; teaching of, 92–
93. See also icnoyot
respeto, and icnoyot, 52
Ricardo, David, 47, 123n24 (ch. 3)
Richardson, Miles, 10, 122n45
(ch. 1)
Ricoeur, Paul, 3, 110, 113, 119n4
(ch. 1), 127nn16,20 (ch. 9),
127nn2–5 (ch. 10), 128nn11–12
(ch. 10)
Ritchie de Key, Mary, 53, 123n2
(ch. 4)
ritual: efficacy of, 81; emotions constructed by, 75; and xochicuahuit
(flower tree), 2. See also Chapter 6
Rodriguez, Luis A., 124n10 (ch. 4)
romantic love, 128n16 (ch. 10); definition of in Spain, 116; Spanish term
for, 5
Rosaldo, Michelle Z., 122n44
(ch. 1)
Rosaldo, Renato, 10, 122n42 (ch. 1)
Rosenblatt, Paul C., 122n42 (ch. 1),
128n16 (ch. 10)
Rosenfeld, Alvin H., 117, 128n26
(ch. 10)
Rovira, Guimar, 121n31 (ch. 1)
Ruiz de Alarcón, Hernando, 107

Sandstrom, Alan, R., viii, 47, 121n36
(ch. 1), 122n3 (ch. 2), 123n5
(ch. 4)
Santiago Chimaltenango, 121n38
(ch. 1)
Scheper-Hughes, Nancy, 111, 114,
121n37 (ch. 1), 127nn23–24
(ch. 9), 128n9 (ch. 10)
school, closing of, 44
Schryer, Frans, 8, 121nn32,35,36
(ch. 1), 122n3 (ch. 2), 123nn12–15
(ch. 3); Huasteca of Hidalgo land
invasions, described by, 44

Scott, James C, 70, 124nn3,5–8 (ch. 5)

sexual loyalties, anxiety about, 100–101

Sherzer, Joel, 120n11 (ch. 1)

Simonelli, Jeanne, 121n31 (ch. 1)

sister: ancient image of, 107; as nahueh, 107–108; as prohibited object, 104

Smith, Adam, 47, 123n24 (ch. 3)

soldiers, as federales, 14

space. *See* cardinal directions, ritual representing; mountains, gender of; quadrilateral view of the universe

Spiro, Melford, 107, 122n44 (ch. 1), 126n6 (ch. 9)

splintering, early signs of, 41

Steiner, George, 122n40 (ch. 1)

Stoler, Ann Laura, 126n3 (ch. 8)

Stoll, David, 45, 121n38 (ch. 1), 123n16 (ch. 3)

structural conditions, for violence, 45

suffering, and compassion, 87

sugar cane, 89–90

Swanson, Guy E., 119n8 (ch. 1)

Tacalot, 11, 86

Taggart, 119n1 (ch. 1), 120nn16,22,23,26 (ch. 1), 121n30 (ch. 1), 123nn19,21 (ch. 3), 125nn12,13,16 (ch. 6), 125n8 (ch. 7), 126nn2,10 (ch. 8), 126nn10–11 (ch. 9), 128n17 (ch. 10)

Talcez, 87, 114; meaning of, 12

Talcuaco, 10; dispute over, 37–38; Dog's home in, 39; invasion of, 2; Juana Gutierrez, former owner of, 36; location of, 11; meaning of, 1; UCI working on, 14

Talcuaco cornfield: army chopping down, 43; Coyote claiming ownership of, 38; Coyote's family chopping down, 43; Wolf's family chopping down, 43

Tallensi, 116

Taltempan: invasion of, 2; Nacho's account of UCI working on, 14

Taltzintan: meaning of, 53; Nacho's father born in, 86

Tamoanchan, 6, 73

tapopoxhuiqueh (incense carrier), 79, 81

Taussig, Michael T., 121n31 (ch. 1)

tazohtaliz (love): as desire, 99; metaphor for, 87; from mother, 86–87; Nacho felt for Victoria, 110; Nacho felt from Victoria, 110–111; Nacho's memories of, 114; spread by ritual, 2; and tequit (work), 87, 90–91, 116; and transference, 114

teicneliliz (compassion), 87; meaning of, 101

Teotihuacan, 7, 73

tequit (work), and tazohtaliz (love), 87, 90–91, 116

testimony, 3. *See also* neixcuitil

Tetela de Ocampo, 11; settlers from, 38

Thanatos, 114

Thomson, Guy P. C., 36, 122nn1–4 (ch. 3)

time, Nahuat conception of, 71

tlazohtaliz (love), in Molina's dictionary, 4

Tonacacihuatl (Our Lady of the Flesh), 73

Tonacateuctli (Our Lord of the Flesh), 73

Topiltzin Quetzalcoatl, 107

Totonac, 1, 80

Totutla, 88

town hall: Coyote's man as president of, 16; president killed by UCI, 16; Rake as president of, 15; UCI attacks officials of, 44

tragedy, 9; definition of, 122n40 (ch. 1)

transference, 94, 113–114

Treatise on Superstitions, 107

trickster tales. *See* "Rabbit and Coyote"

Trinity, and flower tree (xochicuahuit), 75

Turner, Jonathan H., 122n41 (ch. 1)

Tzinacapan, 125n15 (ch. 6)

UCI: acronym for, 1; allies of, 41–42; appearing in Huitzilan, 8, 14, 39; as armed band, 66; arms, sources of, 48–49; as Nahuat group, 49; background of, 8; clashing with Wolf, 14; compared to EZLN, 8; confronting Wolf's brother, 49–52; enemies of, 41–42; federales pursuing, 14; headquarters of, 42; leader, shooting of, 43; Lucio Cabañas, extolled by, 43; meetings held by, 40; mestizos, relations with, 49–53; Nacho's father-in-law joining, 15; organization of, 56; Pahuatla, in, 8; size of, 56; slogans broadcast by, 53; state militia pursuing, 41; town hall officials attacked by, 16, 43–44; working on Talcuaco, 41; Zapata evoked by, 42

Uno más Uno, 124nn8,10 (ch. 4)

van den Berghe, Pierre, 123n1 (ch. 4)
Vansina, Jan, 119n8 (ch. 1)
Velasco Toro, José, 122n2 (ch. 3)
Victoria: children of, 25; daughter grieving, 28–30; death of, 22–24; father of, dying, 59–60; father of, helping Nacho, 16; father of, joining UCI, 15, 17–18; language spoken by, 36–37; loved by Nacho, 110; Nacho feeling love from, 110–111; Ponciano Bonilla, as granddaughter of, 37; saving Nacho from Wrath, 19, 111
Villa Rojas, Alfonso, 122n2 (ch. 3)
violence: explanation of, 48; structural conditions of, 45

Walsh, Patricia, 122n42 (ch. 1)
War of the Castes, 36, 122n2 (ch. 3)
Watanabe, John M., 121n38 (ch. 1)
Weisman, Gary, 119nn5,9 (ch. 1)
White, Hayden, 122n41 (ch. 1), 124n11 (ch. 5)

Whittaker, Gordon, 126n9 (ch. 9)
Winnebago, 120n10 (ch. 1)
witch, Nahuat word for, 63
witchcraft: killings attributed to, 63–64; Nahuat view of, 62–63
Wolf: as ally of Coyote, 49; as enemy of Dog, 39; as enemy of UCI, 14; as enemy of Wrath, 39; evades UCI attackers, 49–52; family of, chopping down cornfield, 43; pseudonym of, 14; shot by UCI, 43
woman: and food, 6; sexual loyalties of, 100–101; split images of, 101; unfaithful, 99–100
Woodrick, Anne C., 112, 127n26 (ch. 9)
work, and love, 90–91, 116. *See also* tequit
Wrath, dispute with Wolf, 39

Xalacapan, 53
Xinachapan, 41
xochicozcat, 73, 77, 82, 85. *See also* flower necklace
xochicuahuit, 73, 77, 80; and "Adam and Eve," 75; Nacho's interpretation of, 77–79; origin of, 2, 73–74; photo of, 74; ritual of, 2; and Trinity, 75; Tzinacapan, in, 125n15 (ch. 6). *See also* flower tree
Xochiquetzal, 6, 73–74
Xochitlan, 80

Yaonáhuac, 7

Zacapoaxtla, 53
Zapata, Emiliano: school curricula, in, 122n6 (ch. 3); UCI use of, 3, 42
Zapatistas, 8
Zapotitlan, 11, 88
Zerubavel, Eviatar, 124n10 (ch. 5)
Zongozotla, 80
Zur, Judith, 9, 112, 121n37 (ch.1), 122n39 (ch. 1), 127nn27–28 (ch. 9)